INDIAN CURRENCY AND FINANCE

INDIAN CURRENCY AND FINANCE

By

JOHN MAYNARD KEYNES

GYAN

Published by

GYAN

Gyan Publishing House
5, Ansari Road
Daryaganj, New Delhi-110002
Phone: 011-47034999, 9811692060
E-mail: books@gyanbooks.com

Distribution Network
gyanbooks.com
India, USA, Canada, UK, Australia, France

ISBN : 978-81-212-9818-6 (PB)
First Published, 1913

2nd Impression 2023

Printed at: Gyan Press, Delhi.

INDIAN CURRENCY AND FINANCE
Author: JOHN MAYNARD KEYNES

INDIAN CURRENCY AND FINANCE

BY

JOHN MAYNARD KEYNES

FELLOW OF KING'S COLLEGE, CAMBRIDGE

1913

PREFACE

When all but the last of the following chapters were already in type, I was offered a seat on the Royal Commission (1913) on Indian Finance and Currency. If my book had been less far advanced, I should, of course, have delayed publication until the Commission had reported, and my opinions had been more fully formed by the discussions of the Commission and by the evidence placed before it. In the circumstances, however, I have decided to publish immediately what I had already written, without the addition of certain other chapters which had been projected. The book, as it now stands, is wholly prior in date to the labours of the Commission.

J. M. KEYNES.

King's College, Cambridge
12*th May* 1913.

CONTENTS

CHAPTER I

CHAPTER II

CHAPTER III

CHAPTER IV

CHAPTER V

CHAPTER VI

CHAPTER VII

CHAPTER VIII

CHAPTER I

THE PRESENT POSITION OF THE RUPEE

1. On the broad historical facts relating to Indian currency, I do not intend to spend time. It is sufficiently well known that until 1893 the currency of India was on the basis of silver freely minted, the gold value of the rupee fluctuating with the gold value of silver bullion. By the depreciation in the gold value of silver, extending over a long period of years, trade was inconvenienced, and Public Finance, by reason of the large payments which the Government must make in sterling, gravely disturbed; until in 1893, after the breakdown of negotiations for bimetallism, the Indian Mints were closed to the free mintage of silver, and the value of the rupee divorced from the value of the metal contained in it. By withholding new issues of currency, the Government had succeeded by 1899 in raising the gold value of the rupee to 1s. 4d., at which figure it has remained without sensible variation ever since.

2. There can be no doubt that at first the Government of India did not fully understand the nature of

the new system; and that several minor mistakes were made at its inception. But few are now found who dispute on broad general grounds the wisdom of the change from a silver to a gold standard.

Time has muffled the outcries of the silver interests, and time has also dealt satisfactorily with what were originally the principal grounds of criticism, namely,—

(1) that the new system was unstable,

(2) that a depreciating currency is advantageous to a country's foreign trade.

3. The second of these complaints was urged with great persistency in 1893. The depreciating rupee acted, it was said, as a bounty to exporters; and the introduction of a gold standard, so it was argued, would greatly injure the export trade in tea, corn, and manufactured cotton. It was plainly pointed out by theorists at the time (*a*) that the advantage to exporters was largely at the expense of other members of the community and could not profit the country as a whole, and (*b*) that it could only be temporary.

The recent spell of rising prices in India has shown clearly in how many ways a depreciating currency damages large sections of the community, although it may temporarily benefit other sections. In fact, some recent complaints against the existing currency policy have been occasioned by the tendency of prices to rise; whereas it is plain that the great change of 1893 must have tended to make them fall, and that rupee prices would, in all probability, be higher than they now are, if the change had not been effected.

With regard to the temporary nature of the effect on exporters, experience has decisively supported theory. The nature of this experience was admirably summed up by Mr. J. B. Brunyate in the Legislative Council (February 25, 1910), speaking in reply to the similar line of argument brought forward by the Bombay mill-owning interests in connexion with the imposition in 1910 of a duty on silver.[1]

[1] Mr. Brunyate spoke as follows:—"Many here will remember the arguments used on behalf of the tea-planting industry. At that time India and China had been competing together for years on the same footing as regards currency. It was argued that the disturbance of the exchange, the appreciation of the rupee and the depreciation of silver, might not only result in India's ascendancy in regard to tea being wrested from her, but in the entire and irretrievable ruin of the tea industry. I am quoting the words actually used by the Darjeeling Planters' Association in 1892. In the year before the closing of the Mints India exported 115 million pounds of tea to foreign countries, and by 1909 had a little more than doubled that amount. Almost exactly the same arguments were used in regard to the cotton industry, and here I must enter into more detail. What the mill-owners feared, and had excellent reason for fearing, was an enormous depreciation in silver. This actually took place. In 1892-93, the year before the Mints were closed, the average value of silver per ounce was nearly 40d. The next year it fell to 33¾d.; the year after to about 29d.; and it stayed at or below 30d. for some years. Surely here were the conditions in which a disastrous stimulus to production in China might have been expected. The so-called bounty in this case was not 2 per cent but 25 per cent. It was not a temporary decline which might be counterbalanced by other causes in the course of a single month. It continued for years, and as we all know silver has not since returned to a price anything like 40d. an ounce. In addition, just before the closing of the Mints occurred there had been considerable over-trading, and the mills had actually been working short time for some months before to enable the Chinese markets to dispose of their accumulated stocks. There was, as a matter of fact, a fall in exports in 1893-94 partly due to the dislocation arising from the changes in our currency system and partly to the existing glut of the Chinese market. The exports picked up, however, in 1894-95, and it would appear that the adjustment of prices and wages in

4. The criticisms of 1893, therefore, are no longer heard, and the Currency Problems with which we are now confronted are new. The evolution of the Indian currency system since 1899 has been rapid, though silent. There have been few public pronouncements of policy on the part of Government, and the legislative changes have been inconsiderable. Yet a system has been developed, which was contemplated neither by those who effected nor by those who opposed the closing of the Mints in 1893, and which was not favoured either by the Government or by the Fowler Committee in 1899, although something like it was suggested at that time. It is not possible to point to any one date at which the currency policy now in force was deliberately adopted.

The fact that the Government of India have drifted into a system and have never set it forth plainly is partly responsible for a widespread misunderstanding of its true character. But this economy of explanation, from which the system has suffered in the past, does

China to the extraordinary new conditions began very quickly, for I find it stated that by the first month of 1894 the mills were again working steadily and profitably. I may perhaps give the actual figures. In 1891-92 the exports of yarn had been 161 million pounds. In 1892-93 the inflated year just preceding the closing of the Mints, they rose to 189 million pounds. In 1893-94 they fell (as I have said) to 134 millions, but went up again the following year to 159 millions. In 1902-3 and 1903-4, though by this time the value of silver had now fallen to 24d., the exports were about 250,000,000 pounds, and in 1905-6 they reached the record figure of 298 millions. In the last two or three years there has been a falling off, owing to various causes, but the amount exported in 1908-9 was as much as 235 millions, and in the exports to China in particular there was a marked improvement."

not make it any the worse intrinsically. The prophecy made before the Committee of 1898 by Mr. A. M. Lindsay, in proposing a scheme closely similar in principle to that which was eventually adopted, has been largely fulfilled. "This change," he said, "will pass unnoticed, except by the intelligent few, and it is satisfactory to find that by this almost imperceptible process the Indian currency will be placed on a footing which Ricardo and other great authorities have advocated as the best of all currency systems, viz., one in which the currency media used in the internal circulation are confined to notes and cheap token coins, which are made to act precisely as if they were bits of gold by being made convertible into gold for foreign payment purposes."

5. In 1893 four possible bases of currency seemed to hold the field: debased and depreciating currencies usually of paper; silver; bimetallism; and gold. It was not to be supposed that the Government of India intended to adopt the first; the second they were avowedly upsetting; the third they had attempted, and had failed, to obtain by negotiation. It seemed to follow that their ultimate objective must be the last—namely, a currency of gold. The Committee of 1892 did not commit themselves; but the system which their recommendations established was generally supposed to be transitional and a first step towards the introduction of gold. The Committee of 1898 explicitly declared themselves to be

in favour of the eventual establishment of a gold currency.

This goal, if it was their goal, the Government of India have never attained. The rupee is still the principal medium of exchange and is of unlimited legal tender. There is no legal enactment compelling any authority to redeem rupees with gold. The fact that since 1899 the gold value of the rupee has only fluctuated within narrow limits is solely due to administrative measures which the Government are under no compulsion to undertake. What, then, is the present position of the rupee?

6. The main features of the Indian system as now established are as follows:—

(1) The rupee is unlimited legal tender and, so far as the law provides, inconvertible.

(2) The sovereign is unlimited legal tender at £1 to 15 rupees, and is convertible at this rate, so long as a Notification issued in 1893 is not withdrawn, *i.e.*, the Government can be required to give 15 rupees in exchange for £1.

(3) As a matter of administrative practice, the Government is, as a rule, willing to give sovereigns for rupees at this rate; but the practice is sometimes suspended and large quantities of gold cannot always be obtained in India by tendering rupees.

(4) As a matter of administrative practice, the Government will sell in Calcutta, in return for rupees tendered there, bills payable in London in sterling

at a rate not more unfavourable than 1s. $3\frac{29}{32}$d. per rupee.

The fourth of these provisions is the vital one for supporting the sterling value of the rupee; and, although the Government have given no binding undertaking to maintain it, a failure to do so might fairly be held to involve an utter breakdown of their system.

Thus the second provision prevents the sterling value of the rupee from rising above 1s. 4d. by more than the cost of remitting sovereigns to India, and the fourth provision prevents it from falling below 1s. $3\frac{29}{32}$d. This means in practice that the extreme limits of variation of the sterling value of the rupee are 1s. $4\frac{1}{8}$d. and 1s. $3\frac{29}{32}$d.

7. The important characteristics of the Indian system are so much a matter of notification and administrative practice that it is impossible to point to single Acts which have made the system what it is. But the following list of dates may be useful for purposes of reference :—

1892. Herschell Committee on Indian Currency.

1893. Act closing the Indian mints to the coinage of silver on private account. Notifications by Government fixing the rate, at which rupees or notes would be supplied in exchange for the tender of gold, at the equivalent of 1s. 4d. the rupee.

1898. Fowler Committee on Indian Currency. Exchange value of rupee touched 1s. 4d.

1899. Act declaring the British sovereign legal tender at 1s. 4d. to the rupee.

1899–1903. Negotiations for coinage of sovereigns in India (dropt indefinitely Feb. 6, 1903).

1900. Gold Standard Reserve instituted out of profits of coinage.

1904. Secretary of State's notification of his willingness to sell Council Bills on India at 1s. $4\frac{1}{8}$d. the rupee without limit.

1905. Act authorising the establishment of the Currency Chest of "earmarked" gold at the Bank of England as part of the Currency Reserve against notes,[1] and the investment of a stated part of the Currency Reserve in sterling securities.

1906. The Notification withdrawn which had directed the issue of rupees against the tender of gold (as distinguished from British gold coin).

1907. Rupee branch of the Gold Standard Reserve instituted.

1908. Sterling drafts sold in Calcutta on London at 1s. $3\frac{29}{32}$d. the rupee, and cashed out of funds from the Gold Standard Reserve.

1910. Act rendering Currency notes of Rs. 10 and 50 universal legal tender,[2] and directing the issue of notes in exchange for British gold coins.

1913. Royal Commission on Indian Finance and Currency.

8. In § 6 I have stated the practical effect of these successive measures. But the legal position is so complicated and peculiar, that it will be worth while to state it quite precisely. Previous to 1893 the Government were bound by the Coinage Act of 1870 to issue rupees, weight for weight, in exchange for silver bullion. There was also in force a Notification of the Governor-General in Council, dating from 1868,

[1] There had been temporary Acts to the same effect in 1898 and 1900.

[2] Notes of Rs. 100 were universalised in 1911 by Notification under this Act.

by which sovereigns were received at Government Treasuries as the equivalent of ten rupees and four annas. This Notification, which had superseded a Notification of 1864 fixing the exchange at ten rupees, had long been inoperative (as the gold exchange value of ten rupees four annas had fallen much below a sovereign). The Act of 1893 was merely a repealing Act, necessary in order to do away with those provisions of the Act of 1870 which provided for the free mintage of silver into rupees. At the same time (1893) the Notification of 1868 was superseded by a new Notification fixing fifteen rupees as the rate at which sovereigns would be accepted at Government Treasuries; and a Notification was issued under the Paper Currency Act of 1882, directing the issue of currency notes in exchange for gold at the Rs. 15 to £1 ratio. The direct issue of rupees against the tender of gold also has been regulated by a series of Notifications, of which the first was published in 1893, up to 1906 rupees being issued against either gold coin or gold bullion; and since 1906 against sovereigns and half-sovereigns only. Apart from Notifications, an Act of 1899 declared British sovereigns legal tender at the Rs. 15 to £1 ratio, an indirect effect of which was to make it possible for Government, so far as Acts are concerned, to redeem notes in gold coin and refuse silver. And lastly, the Paper Currency Act of 1910 bound the Government to issue notes against the tender of British gold coin,

The convertibility of the sovereign into rupees at the Rs. 15 to £1 ratio is not laid down, therefore, in any Act whatever. It depends on Notifications withdrawable by the Executive at will. Further, the management of the Gold Standard Reserve is governed neither by Act nor by Notification, but by administrative practice solely; and the sale of Council Bills on India and of sterling drafts on London is regulated by announcements changeable at administrative discretion from time to time.

All this emphasises the gradual nature of the system's growth, and the transitional character of existing legislation. As matters now are, there is something to be said for a new Act, which, while leaving administrative discretion free where there is still good ground for this, might consolidate and clarify the position.

9. As a result of these various measures, the rupee remains the local currency in India, but the Government take precautions for ensuring its convertibility into international currency at an approximately stable rate. The stability of the Indian system depends upon their keeping sufficient reserves of coined rupees to enable them at all times to exchange international currency for local currency; and sufficient liquid resources in sterling to enable them to change back the local currency into international currency, whenever they are required to do so. The special features of the system, although, as we shall

see later, these features are not in fact by any means peculiar to India, are: first, that the actual medium of exchange is a local currency distinct from the international currency; second, that the Government is more ready to redeem the local currency (rupees) in bills payable in international currency (gold) at a foreign centre (London) than to redeem it outright locally; and third, that the Government, having taken on itself the responsibility for providing local currency in exchange for international currency and for changing back local currency into international currency when required, must keep two kinds of reserves, one for each of these purposes.

I will deal with these characteristics in successive chapters. It is convenient to begin with the second of them and at the outset to discuss in a general way the system of currency, of which the Indian is the most salient example, known to students as the *Gold-Exchange Standard.* Then we will take the first of them in Chapters III. and IV. on *Paper Currency* and on the *Present Position of Gold in India and Proposals for a Gold Currency*; and the third in Chapter VI. on the *Secretary of State's Reserves.*

10. But before we pass to these several features of the Indian system, it will be worth while to emphasise two respects in which this system is *not* peculiar. In the first place a system, in which the rupee is maintained at 1s. 4d. by regulation, does not affect

the level of prices differently from the way in which it would be affected by a system in which the rupee was a gold coin worth 1s. 4d., except in a very indirect and unimportant way to be explained in a moment. So long as the rupee is worth 1s. 4d. in gold, no merchant or manufacturer considers of what material it is made when he fixes the price of his product. The *indirect* effect on prices, due to the rupee's being silver, is similar to the effect of the use of any medium of exchange, such as cheques or notes, which economises the use of gold. If the use of gold is economised in any country, gold throughout the world is less valuable—gold prices, that is to say, are higher. But as this effect is shared by the whole world, the effect on prices in any country of economies in the use of gold made by that country is likely to be relatively slight. In short, a policy which led to a greater use of gold in India would tend, by increasing the demand for gold in the world's markets, somewhat to lower the level of world prices as measured in gold; but it would not cause any alteration worth considering in the *relative* rates of exchange of Indian and non-Indian commodities.

In the second place, although it is true that the maintenance of the rupee at or near 1s. 4d. is due to regulation, it is not true, when once 1s. 4d. rather than some other gold value has been determined, that the volume of currency in circulation depends in the least upon the policy of the Government or the caprice of an official.[1] This part of the system is as perfectly automatic as in any other country The Government has put itself under an obligation to supply rupees whenever sovereigns are tendered, and it often permits or encourages the tender of sovereigns in London as well as in India; but it has no power or opportunity of forcing rupees into circulation otherwise. In two matters only does the Government use a discretionary power. First, in order that it may always be possible to fulfil this obligation, it is necessary to keep a certain reserve of coined rupees, just as some authority in this country—in point of fact the Bank of England—must keep some reserve of token silver and coined sovereigns and not hold in its vaults too large a proportion of uncoined or foreign gold. The magnitude of this reserve is within the discretion of the Indian Government. To a certain extent they must anticipate probable demands on the output of the Mint. But if they miscalculate and mint more than they need, the new rupees must lie in the Government's own chests until they are wanted, and the date at which they emerge into circulation it is beyond the power of the Government to determine. In the second

[1] The Hon. Mr. Dadabhoy, speaking in the Legislative Council in 1910, argued that "the harmful effects of a further fall in silver (*i.e.* in its bullion value) can be neutralised by Government by creating a further contraction in the volume of the currency, and thus producing a greater scarcity of the rupee, by maintaining the Gold Standard Reserve at a higher figure, and, further, by more frequent withdrawal of Council Bills from the market." A contraction of the currency would not, of course, have the effect supposed, but the Government could not, in fact, bring about a contraction in the manner described.

place, the Government can postpone for a short time a demand for rupees by refusing to supply them in return for sovereigns tendered in London and by insisting upon the sovereigns being sent to Calcutta. Sometimes they do this, but very often it is worth their while, for reasons to be explained in detail later on, to accept the tender of sovereigns in London. In either of these cases the permanent effect of their action one way or the other on the volume of circulation is inconsiderable. The kind of difference it makes is comparable to the difference which would be made if it lay within the discretion of a government to charge or not, as it saw fit, a small *brassage* not much greater than the cost of coining.[1]

[1] This question of the power of Government over the volume of circulation is discussed in much greater detail in § 8 of Chapter V.

CHAPTER II

THE GOLD-EXCHANGE STANDARD

1. If we are to see the Indian system in its proper perspective, it is necessary to digress for a space to a discussion of currency evolution in general.

My purpose is, first, to show that the British system is peculiar and is not suited to other conditions; second, that the conventional idea of "sound" currency is chiefly derived from certain superficial aspects of the British system; third, that a somewhat different type of system has been developed in most other countries; and fourth, that in essentials the system which has been evolved in India conforms to this foreign type. I shall be concerned throughout this chapter with the general characteristics of currency systems, not with the details of their working.

2. The history of currency, so far as it is relevant to our present purpose, virtually begins with the nineteenth century. During the second quarter of this century England was alone in possessing an orthodox "sound" currency on a gold basis. Gold was the sole standard of value; it circulated freely

from hand to hand; and it was freely available for export. Up to 1844 bank notes showed a tendency to become a formidable rival to gold as the actual medium of exchange. But the Bank Act of that year set itself to hamper this tendency and to encourage the use of gold as the medium of exchange as well as the standard of value. This Act was completely successful in stopping attempts to economise gold by the use of notes. But the Bank Act did nothing to hinder the use of cheques, and the very remarkable development of this medium of exchange during the next fifty years led in this country, without any important development in the use of notes or tokens, to a monetary organisation more perfectly adapted for the economy of gold than any which exists elsewhere. In this matter of the use of cheques Great Britain has been followed by the rest of the English-speaking world — Canada, Australia, South Africa, and the United States of America. But in other countries currency evolution has been, chiefly, along different lines.

3. In the early days of banking of the modern type in England, gold was not infrequently required to meet runs on banks by their depositors, who were always liable in difficult times to fall into a state of panic lest they should be unable to withdraw their deposits in case of real need. With the growth of the stability of banking, and especially with the growth of confidence in this stability amongst

depositors, these occasions have become more and more infrequent, and many years have now passed since there has been any run of dangerous proportions on English banks. Gold reserves, therefore, in Great Britain are no longer held primarily with a view to emergencies of this kind. The uses of gold coin in Great Britain are now three—as the medium of exchange for certain kinds of out-of-pocket expenditure, such as that on railway travelling, for which custom requires cash payment; for the payment of wages; and to meet a drain of specie abroad.

Fluctuations in the demand for gold in the first two uses are of secondary importance, and can usually be predicted with a good deal of accuracy,—at holiday seasons, at the turn of the quarter, at the end of the week, at harvest. Fluctuations in the demand in the third use are of greater magnitude and, apart from the regular autumn drain, not so easily foreseen. Our gold reserve policy is mainly dictated, therefore, by considerations arising out of the possible demand for export.

To guard against a possible drain of gold abroad, a complicated mechanism has been developed which in the details of its working is peculiar to this country. A drain of gold can only come about if foreigners choose to turn into gold claims, which they have against us for immediate payment, and we have no counterbalancing claims against them for equally immediate payment. The drain can only be stopped if we can rapidly bring to bear our counterbalancing claims. When we come to consider how this can best be done, it is to be noticed that the position of a country which is preponderantly a creditor in the international short-loan market is quite different from that of a country which is preponderantly a debtor. In the former case, which is that of Great Britain, it is a question of reducing the amount lent; in the latter case it is a question of increasing the amount borrowed. A machinery which is adapted for action of the first kind may be ill suited for action of the second. Partly as a consequence of this, partly as a consequence of the peculiar organisation of the London Money Market, the "bank rate" policy for regulating the outflow of gold has been admirably successful in this country, and yet cannot stand elsewhere unaided by other devices. It is not necessary for the purposes of this survey to consider precisely how changes in the bank rate affect the balance of immediate indebtedness. It will be sufficient to say that it tends to hamper the brokers, who act as middlemen between the British short-loan fund and the foreign demand for accommodation (chiefly materialised in the offer of bills for discount), and to cause them to enter into a less volume of new business than that of the short loans formerly contracted and now falling due, thus bringing to bear the necessary counterbalancing claims against foreign countries.

4. The essential characteristics of the British

monetary system are, therefore, the use of cheques as the principal medium of exchange, and the use of the bank rate for regulating the balance of immediate foreign indebtedness (and hence the flow, by import and export, of gold).

5. The development of foreign monetary systems into their present shapes began in the last quarter of the nineteenth century. At that time London was at the height of her financial supremacy, and her monetary arrangements had stood the test of time and experience. Foreign systems, therefore, were greatly influenced at their inception by what were regarded as the fundamental tenets of the British system. But foreign observers seem to have been more impressed by the fact that the Englishman had sovereigns in his pocket than by the fact that he had a cheque-book in his desk; and took more notice of the "efficacy" of the bank rate and of the deliberations of the Court of Directors on Thursdays, than of the peculiar organisation of the brokers and the London Money Market, and of Great Britain's position as a creditor nation. They were thus led to imitate the form rather than the substance. When they introduced the gold standard, they set up gold currencies as well; and in several cases an official bank rate was established on the British model. Germany led the way in 1871–73. Even now apologists of the Reichsbank will sometimes speak as if its bank rate were efficacious by itself in the same manner as the

Bank of England's. But, in fact, the German system, though ostensibly modelled in part upon the British system, has become, by force of circumstances, essentially different.

It is not necessary for this survey to consider individual systems in any detail. But, confining ourselves to European countries, whether we consider, for example, France, Austria-Hungary, Russia, Italy, Sweden, or Holland, while most of these countries have a gold currency and an official Bank Rate, in none of them is gold the principal medium of exchange, and in none of them is the bank rate their only habitual support against an outward drain of gold.

6. With the use of substitutes for gold I will deal in Chapter IV. in treating of the proper position of gold in the Indian system. But what props are commonly brought to the support of an "ineffective" Bank Rate in countries other than Great Britain? Roughly speaking, there are three. A very large gold reserve may be maintained, so that a substantial drain on it may be faced with equanimity; free payments in gold may be partially suspended; or foreign credits and bills may be kept which can be drawn upon when necessary. The Central Banks of most European countries depend (in varying degrees) upon all three.

The Bank of France uses the first two,[1] and her

[1] For example, in November 1912, "no gold was handed across the counter at the Bank of France except on the most urgent demand, and then

holdings of foreign bills are not, at normal times, important.[1] Her bank rate is not fixed primarily with a view to foreign conditions, and a change in it is usually intended to affect home affairs (though these may of course depend and react on foreign affairs).

Germany is in a state of transition, and her present position is avowedly unsatisfactory. The theory of her arrangements seems to be that she depends on her bank rate after the British model; but in practice her bank rate is not easily rendered effective, and must usually be reinforced by much unseen pressure by the Reichsbank on the other elements of the money market. Her gold reserve is not large enough for the first expedient to be used lightly. Free payment in gold is sometimes, in effect, partially suspended,[2] though covertly and with

---

the highest sum paid in gold was 300 francs per head. The other banks followed this example, and the most generous released 200 francs in gold. All special wishes for payment in money were charged 1 per cent premium. At the same time, deposits in gold were credited with 1 per cent premium" (see *Bankers' Magazine*, December 1912, p. 794). At the beginning of the month cashiers were charging a premium or commission of 6 f. per 1000 f. for payments in gold instead of silver (see *Economist*, November 9, 1912, p. 961).

[1] Although the Bank of France only holds an important quantity of foreign bills (generally sterling), on exceptional occasions, *e.g.* at the beginning and end of 1907 and at the end of 1909, foreign paper enters very largely, through the agency of the great Crédit Banks, into the transactions of the French Money Market. These institutions take foreign bills into their own portfolios, and obtain the necessary funds by rediscounting inland bills at the Bank of France. Thus the French mechanism is much more closely analogous to the British than appears outwardly, and the influence of the Bank of France, like that of the Bank of England, is mainly indirect. The possibility of this is no doubt due to the fact that France, like Great Britain, is a creditor nation in the international short-loan market.

[2] For example, in November 1912 there was a premium of nearly ¾ per cent on gold for export.

shame. To an increasing extent the Reichsbank depends on variations in her holding of foreign bills and credits. A few years ago such holdings were of small importance. The table given below shows with what rapidity the part taken by foreign bills and credits in the finance of the Reichsbank has been growing. The authorities of the Reichsbank have now learnt that their position in the international short-loan market is not one which permits them to fix the bank rate and then idly to await the course of events.

REICHSBANK'S HOLDINGS OF FOREIGN BILLS (EXCLUDING CREDITS).

	Average for Year.	Maximum.	Minimum.
1895	£120,000	£152,000	£100,000
1900	1,270,000	3,540,000	160,000
1905	1,580,000	2,490,000	970,000
1906	2,060,000	2,990,000	830,000
1907	2,223,000	3,000,000	1,130,000
1908	3,544,000	6,366,000	977,800
1909	5,362,000	7,978,000	2,824,800
1910[1]	7,032,000	8,855,000	4,893,300

[1] Since 1910 these figures have not been stated in the Reichsbank's annual reports.

REICHSBANK'S HOLDINGS OF FOREIGN BILLS AND CREDITS WITH FOREIGN CORRESPONDENTS ON LAST DAY OF EACH YEAR.

31st Dec.	Bills.	Credits.	Total.
1906	£3,209,000	£993,000	£4,202,000
1907	1,289,000	503,000	1,792,000
1908	6,457,000	1,234,000	7,691,000
1909	6,000,000	3,369,000	9,369,000
1910	8,114,000	4,205,000	12,309,000
1911	7,114,000	1,439,000	8,553,000
1912	...	...	...

7. If we pass from France, whose position as a creditor country is not altogether unlike Great Britain's, and from Germany, which is at any rate able to do a good deal towards righting the balance of immediate indebtedness by the sale of securities having an international market, to other countries of less financial strength, we find the dependence of their Central Banks on holdings of foreign bills and on foreign credits, their willingness to permit a premium on gold, and the inadequacy of their bank rates taken by themselves, to be increasingly marked. I will first mention very briefly one or two salient facts, and will then consider their underlying meaning, always with an ultimate view to their bearing on the affairs of India.

8. To illustrate how rare a thing in Europe a perfect and automatic gold standard is, let us take the most recent occasion of stringency—November 1912. The Balkan War was at this time at an acute stage, but the European situation was only moderately anxious. Compared with the crisis at the end of 1907, the financial position was one of comparative calm. Yet in the course of that month there was a premium on gold of about $\frac{3}{4}$ per cent in France, Germany, Russia, Austria-Hungary,[1] and Belgium. So high a premium as this is as effective in retaining gold as a very considerable addition to the bank rate.

[1] This premium was made possible by the Austro-Hungarian Bank's exercising its right to refuse to exchange its bank notes for gold freely.

If, for example, the premium did not last more than three months, it would add to the profits of a temporary deposit of funds for that period as much as an addition of 3 per cent to the discount rate; or, to put it the other way round, there would need to be an additional profit of 3 per cent elsewhere if it were to be worth while to send funds abroad.

9. The growing importance of foreign bills in the portfolios of the Reichsbank has been shown above. The importance of foreign bills and credits in the policy of the Austro-Hungarian Bank is of longer standing and is better known. They always form an important part of its reserves, and the part first utilised in times of stringency.[1] It was supposed that in the third quarter of 1911 the Bank placed not less than £4,000,000 worth of gold bills at the disposal of the Austro-Hungarian market in order to support exchange. Amongst European countries, Russia now keeps the largest aggregate of funds in foreign bills and in balances abroad—amounting in November 1912 to £26,630,000.[2] Account being taken of their total resources, however, the banks of the three Scandinavian countries, Sweden, Norway, and Denmark, hold the

[1] In the abnormal conditions of recent times (1912–13), however, the Bank has not found it possible to maintain this part of its reserves at a high level.

[2] This does not include the funds held abroad on account of the Russian Treasury. Speaking in March 1913, in the Budget Committee of the Duma, the Minister of Finance stated that the total amount of Russian State funds placed abroad was £60,000,000.

highest proportion in the form of balances abroad—amounting in November 1912, for the three countries in the aggregate, to about £7,000,000. These are enough examples for my purpose.

10. What is the underlying significance of this growing tendency on the part of European State Banks to hold a part of their reserves in foreign bills or foreign credits? We saw above that the bank-rate policy of the Bank of England is successful because by indirect means it causes the Money Market to reduce its short-period loans to foreign countries, and thus to turn the balance of immediate indebtedness in our favour. This indirect policy is less feasible in countries where the Money Market is already a borrower rather than a lender in the international market. In such countries a rise in the bank rate cannot be relied on to produce the desired effect with due rapidity. A direct policy on the part of the Central Bank, therefore, must be employed. If the Money Market is not a lender in the international market, the Bank itself must be at pains to become to some extent one. The Bank of England lends to middlemen who, by holding bills or otherwise, lend abroad. A rise in the bank rate is equivalent to putting pressure on these middlemen to diminish their commitments. In countries where the Money Market is neither so highly developed nor, in relation to foreign countries, so self-supporting, the Central Bank, if it is to be secure, must take the matter

in hand itself and, by itself entering the international money market as a lender at short notice, place itself in funds, at foreign centres, which can be rapidly withdrawn when they are required. The only alternative would be the holding of a much larger reserve of gold, the expense of which would be nearly intolerable. The new method combines safety with economy. Just as individuals have learnt that it is cheaper and not less safe to keep their ultimate reserves on deposit at their bankers than to keep them at home in cash, so the second stage of monetary evolution is now entered on, and nations are learning that *some part* of the cash reserves of their banks (we cannot go further than this at present) may be properly kept on deposit in the international money market. This is not the expedient of second-rate or impoverished countries; it is the expedient of all those who have not attained a high degree of financial supremacy—of all those, in fact, who are not themselves international bankers.

11. In the forty years, therefore, during which the world has been coming on to a gold standard (without, however, giving up for that reason its local currencies of notes or token silver), two devices —apart from the bullion reserve itself and the bank rate—have been evolved for protecting the local currencies. The first is to permit a small variation in the ratio of exchange between the local currency and gold, amounting perhaps to an occasional premium

of $\frac{3}{4}$ per cent on the latter; this may help to tide over a stringency which is seasonal or of short duration without raising to a dangerous level the rate of discount on purely local transactions. The second is for the Government or Central Bank to hold resources available abroad, which can be used for maintaining the gold parity of the local currency, when there is the need for it.

12. We are now more nearly in a position to come back to the currency of India herself, and to see it in its proper relation to those of other countries. At one end of the scale we have Great Britain and France—creditor nations in the short-loan market.[1] In an intermediate position comes Germany—a creditor in relation to many of her neighbours, but apt to be a debtor in relation to France, Great Britain, and the United States. Next come such countries as Russia and Austria-Hungary—rich and powerful, with immense reserves of gold, but debtor nations, dependent in the short-loan market on their neighbours. From the currencies of these it is an easy step to those of the great trading nations of Asia—India, Japan, and the Dutch East Indies.

13. I say that from the currencies of such countries as Russia and Austria-Hungary to those which have

[1] I have throughout deliberately ignored the current practice of the United States in these matters. Her development and present position are anomalous, and have claimed no imitators. Her arrangements would need a discussion to themselves, and would, I think, convey few lessons of value to students of Indian affairs. In dealing with her dependencies, she has herself imitated, almost slavishly, India.

explicitly and in name a Gold-Exchange Standard[1] it is an easy step. The Gold-Exchange Standard is simply a more regularised form of the same system as theirs. In their essential characteristics and in the monetary logic which underlies them the currencies of India and Austria-Hungary (to take these as our examples) are not really different. In India we know the extreme limits of fluctuation in the exchange value of the rupee; we know the precise volume of reserves which the Government holds in gold and in credits abroad; and we know at what moment the Government will step in and utilise these resources for the support of the rupee. In Austria-Hungary the system is less automatic, and the Bank is allowed a wide discretion. In detail, of course, there are a number of differences. India keeps a somewhat higher proportion of her reserves in foreign credits, and keeps some part of these credits in a less liquid form. She also keeps a portion of her gold reserve in London—a practice made possible by the fact that for India London is not strictly a foreign centre. On the other hand, India is probably more willing than the Bank of Austria-Hungary to supply gold on demand. If we are to judge from the experience of

[1] I may seem to speak as if Japan had in name a Gold-Exchange Standard, which is not the case. There is not much publicity in regard to her monetary arrangements. But I believe that they are, in fact, such that it is as a Gold-Exchange Standard hers ought impartially to be classified. The Finance Minister stated in the Diet in 1912 that the gold funds held by the Government and the Bank of Japan in Europe and the United States were about £37,000,000. The amount of gold circulating in Japan herself is, I believe, inconsiderable.

recent years, India inclines to use her gold reserves, Austria-Hungary her foreign credits, first. But in the essentials of the Gold-Exchange Standard—the use of a local currency mainly not of gold, some degree of unwillingness to supply gold locally in exchange for the local currency, but a high degree of willingness to sell foreign exchange for payment in local currency at a certain maximum rate, and to use foreign credits in order to do this—the two countries agree.

14. To say that the Gold - Exchange Standard merely carries somewhat further the currency arrangements which several European countries have evolved during the last quarter of a century is not, of course, to justify it. But if we see that the Gold-Exchange Standard is not, in the currency world of to-day, anomalous, and that it is in the main stream of currency evolution, we shall have a wider experience, on which to draw, in criticising it, and may be in a better position to judge of its details wisely. Much nonsense is talked about a gold standard's properly carrying a gold currency with it. If we mean by a gold currency a state of affairs in which gold is the principal or even, in the aggregate, a very important medium of exchange, no country in the world has such a thing.[1] Gold is an international, but not a local currency. The currency problem of each country is to ensure that they shall run no risk of being

[1] Unless it be Egypt.

unable to put their hands on international currency when they need it, and to waste as small a proportion of their resources on holdings of actual gold as is compatible with this. The proper solution for each country must be governed by the nature of its position in the international money market and of its relations to the chief financial centres, and by those national customs in matters of currency which it may be unwise to disturb. It is as an attempt to solve this problem that the Gold-Exchange Standard ought to be judged.

15. We have been concerned so far with transitional systems of currency. I will conclude this chapter with a brief history in outline of the Gold-Exchange Standard itself. It will then be time to pass from high generalities to the actual details of the Indian system.

The Gold-Exchange Standard arises out of the discovery that, so long as gold is available for payments of *international* indebtedness at an approximately constant rate in terms of the national currency, it is a matter of comparative indifference whether it actually *forms* the national currency.

The Gold-Exchange Standard may be said to exist when gold does not circulate in a country to an appreciable extent, when the local currency is not necessarily redeemable in gold, but when the Government or Central Bank makes arrangements for the provision of foreign remittances in gold at a fixed maximum rate in terms of the local currency, the reserves necessary to provide these remittances being kept to a considerable extent abroad.

A system closely resembling the Gold-Exchange Standard was actually employed during the second half of the eighteenth century for regulating the exchange between London and Edinburgh. Its theoretical advantages were first set forth by Ricardo at the time of the Bullionist Controversy. He laid it down that a currency is in its most perfect state when it consists of a cheap material, but having an equal value with the gold it professes to represent; and he suggested that convertibility for the purposes of the foreign exchanges should be ensured by the tendering on demand of gold *bars* (not coin) in exchange for notes,—so that gold might be available for purposes of export only, and would be prevented from entering into the internal circulation of the country. In an article contributed to the *Contemporary Review* of 1887, Dr. Marshall again brought these advantages to the notice of practical men.

16. The first crude attempt in recent times at establishing a standard of this type was made by Holland. The free coinage of silver was suspended in 1877. But the currency continued to consist mainly of silver and paper. It has been maintained since that date at a constant value in terms of gold by the Bank's regularly providing gold when it is required for export and by its using its authority at the same

time for restricting so far as possible the use of gold at home. To make this policy possible, the Bank of Holland has kept a reserve, of a moderate and economical amount, partly in gold, partly in foreign bills.[1] During the long period for which this policy has been pursued, it has been severely tried more than once, but has stood the test successfully.

It must be noticed, however, that although Holland has kept gold and foreign bills as a means of obtaining a credit abroad at any moment, she has not kept a standing credit in any foreign financial centre. The method of keeping a token currency at a fixed par with gold by means of credit abroad was first adopted by Count Witte for Russia in the transitional period from inconvertible paper to a gold standard;—in the autumn of 1892 the Department of Finance offered to buy exchange on Berlin at 2·18 marks and to sell at 2·20. In the same year (1892) the Austro-Hungarian system, referred to above, was established. As in India their exchange policy was evolved gradually. The present arrangements, which date

[1] In the course of the last twenty years, however, the Bank of Holland, having got rid of the greater part of her redundant stock of silver coins, has gradually come to rely more on her holding of gold and less on her holding of foreign bills than formerly. In 1892–93 foreign bills at £1,801,409 were about 16 per cent of her resources (excluding silver coin); in 1911–12 they had fallen to £1,389,139 or about 5·5 per cent of her resources (excluding silver coin). But the media of exchange are still notes and silver, and not less than formerly does the Bank pursue the policy of keeping her gold for purposes of export only and of withholding it from circulation. Almost the whole of her stock of gold is in the form of bars and foreign coin. (It should be added, however, that at the end of 1912 there were proposals, in order to avoid fresh coinage of silver, for the introduction of a 5 fl. gold piece.)

from 1896, were made possible by the strong preference of the public for notes over gold and by the provision of the law which permitted the holding of foreign bills as cover for the note issue. This exchange policy is the easier, because the Austro-Hungarian Bank is by far the largest dealer in exchange in Vienna;—just as the policy of the Government of India is facilitated by the commanding influence which the system of Council Bills gives it over the exchange market.

17. But although India was not the first country to lead the way to a Gold-Exchange Standard, she was the first to adopt it in a complete form. When in 1893, on the recommendation of the Herschell Committee, following upon the agitation of the Indian Currency Association, the Mints were closed to the free coinage of silver, it was believed that the cessation of coinage and the refusal of the Secretary of State to sell his bills below 1s. 4d. would suffice to establish this ratio of exchange. The Government had not then the experience which we have now; we now know that such measures are not by themselves sufficient, except under the influence of favouring circumstances. As a matter of fact the circumstances were, at first, unfavourable. Exchange fell considerably below 1s. 4d., and the Secretary of State had to sell his bills for what he could get. If there had been, at the existing level of prices, a rapidly expanding demand for currency at the time when the

Mints were closed, the measures actually taken might very well have proved immediately successful. But the demand did not expand, and the very large issues of currency immediately before and just after the closure of the Mints proved sufficient to satisfy the demand for several years to come;—just as a demand for new currency on an abnormally high scale from 1903 to 1907, accompanied by high rates of discount, was followed in 1908 by a complete cessation of demand and a period of comparatively low rates of discount. Favourable circumstances, however, came at last, and by January 1898 exchange was stable at 1s. 4d. The Fowler Committee, then appointed, recommended a gold currency as the ultimate objective. It is since that time that the Government of India have adopted, or drifted into, their present system.

18. The Gold-Exchange Standard in the form in which it has been adopted in India is justly known as the Lindsay scheme. It was proposed and advocated from the earliest discussions, when the Indian currency problem first became prominent, by Mr. A. M. Lindsay, Deputy-Secretary of the Bank of Bengal, who always maintained that "they *must* adopt my scheme despite themselves." His first proposals were made in 1876 and 1878. They were repeated in 1885 and again in 1892, when he published a pamphlet entitled *Ricardo's Exchange Remedy*. Finally, he explained his views in detail to the Committee of 1898.

Lindsay's scheme was severely criticised both by Government officials and leading financiers. Lord Farrer described it as "far too clever for the ordinary English mind with its ineradicable prejudice for an immediately tangible gold backing to all currencies." Lord Rothschild, Sir John Lubbock (Lord Avebury), Sir Samuel Montagu (the late Lord Swaythling) all gave evidence before the Committee that any system without a visible gold currency would be looked on with distrust. Mr. Alfred de Rothschild went so far as to say that "in fact a gold standard without a gold currency seemed to him an utter impossibility." Financiers of this type will not admit the feasibility of anything until it has been demonstrated to them by practical experience. It follows, therefore, that they will seldom give their support to what is new.

19. Since the Indian system has been perfected and its provisions generally known, it has been widely imitated both in Asia and elsewhere. In 1903 the Government of the United States introduced a system avowedly based on it into the Philippines. Since that time it has been established, under the influence of the same Government, in Mexico and Panama. The Government of Siam have adopted it. The French have introduced it in Indo-China. Our own Colonial Office have introduced it in the Straits Settlements and are about to introduce it into the West African Colonies. Something similar has existed in Java under Dutch influences for many years. The

Japanese system is virtually the same in practice. In China, as is well known, currency reform has not yet been carried through. The Gold-Exchange Standard is the only possible means of bringing China on to a gold basis, and the alternative policy (the policy of our own Foreign Office) is to be content at first with a standard, as well as a currency, of silver. A powerful body of opinion, led by the United States, favours the immediate introduction of a gold standard on the Indian model.

It may fairly be said, therefore, that in the last ten years the Gold-Exchange Standard has become the prevailing monetary system of Asia. I have tried to show that it is also closely related to the prevailing tendencies in Europe. Speaking as a theorist, I believe that it contains one essential element—the use of a cheap local currency artificially maintained at par with the international currency or standard of value (whatever that may ultimately turn out to be)—in the ideal currency of the future. But it is now time to turn to details.

CHAPTER III

PAPER CURRENCY

1. THE chief characteristics of the Indian system of currency have been roughly sketched in the first chapter. I will now proceed to a description of the system of note issue.

2. In existing conditions the rupee, being a token coin, is virtually a note printed on silver. The custom and convenience of the people justify this, so far as concerns payment in small sums. But in itself it is extravagant. When rupees are issued, the Government, instead of being able to place to reserve the whole nominal value of the coin, is able to retain only the difference between the nominal value and the cost of the silver.[1] For large payments, therefore, it is important to encourage the use of notes to the utmost extent possible,—from the point of view of economy, because by these means the Government may obtain a large part of the reserves necessary for

[1] The rupee contains $\frac{3}{8}$ oz. of silver of eleven-twelfths fineness. When standard silver is at 24d. per oz. the cost of a rupee to the Government is about 9·181d.; at 32d. per oz. it is about 12·241d. The average rate of profit on coinage of rupees from 1910 to May 1912 was about 42% of the nominal value.

the support of a Gold-Exchange Standard, and also because only thus will it be possible to introduce a proper degree of elasticity in the seasonal supply of currency

3. By Acts of 1839–43 the Presidency Banks of Bengal, Bombay, and Madras were authorised to issue notes payable on demand; but the use of the notes was practically limited to the three Presidency towns.[1] These Acts were repealed in 1861, when the present Government Paper Currency was first instituted. Since that time no banks have been allowed to issue notes in India.

Proposals for a Government Paper Currency were instituted in 1859 by Mr. James Wilson on his going out to India as the first Financial Member.[2] Mr. Wilson died before his scheme could be carried into effect, and the Act setting up the Paper Currency scheme, which became law in 1861, differed in some important respects from his original proposals.[3] The system was eventually set up under the influence of the very rigid ideas as to the proper regulation of note issue prevailing, as a result of the controversies which had culminated in the British Bank Act of 1844, amongst English economists of that time. According to these ideas, the proper principles of note issue

[1] See also pp. 199, 200.

[2] For this and other historical details see J. B. Brunyate, *An Account of the Presidency Banks*.

[3] Mr. Wilson had proposed to invest a high proportion of the reserve (perhaps two-thirds) in Government securities.

were two—first, that the function of note issue should be entirely dissociated from that of banking; and second, that "the amount of notes issued on Government securities should be maintained at a fixed sum, within the limit of the smallest amount which experience has proved to be necessary for the monetary transactions of the country, and that any further amount of notes should be issued on coin or bullion."[1] These principles were orthodox and all others "unsound." "The sound principle for regulating the issue of a Paper Circulation," wrote the Secretary of State, "is that which was enforced on the Bank of England by the Act of 1844." In England, of course, bankers immediately set themselves to recover the economy and elasticity, which the Act of 1844 banished from the English system, by other means; and with the development of the cheque system to its present state of perfection they have magnificently succeeded. In foreign countries all kinds of new principles have been tried for the regulation of note issue, and some of them have been very successful. In India the creed of 1861 is still repeated; but by unforeseen chance the words have changed their meanings, and have permitted the old system to acquire through inadvertence a certain degree of usefulness. The coin, in which the greater part of the reserve had to

[1] I quote this from the Secretary of State's despatch (Sir Charles Wood, March 26, 1860) criticising Mr. Wilson's original scheme.

be held, was, of course, the rupee. In 1861 this was a freely minted coin worth no more than its bullion value. When the rupee became an artificially valued token, rupees tacitly remained the legitimate form of the reserve (although after a time sovereigns were added as an optional alternative). Thus the authorities are free, if they like, to hold the whole of the Currency Reserve in rupee-tokens, and this reserve has become, therefore (as we shall see below), an important part of the mechanism by which the supply of silver rupees to the currency is duly regulated. While, however, the note issue has managed to evolve an important function for itself, I think the time has come when the usefulness of the Currency Reserve may be much increased by a deliberate consideration of the place it might fill in the organism of the Indian Money Market. I return to this later in the chapter. In the meantime I pass to a description of the Paper Currency as it now is —insisting, however, that when we come to consider how it may be improved, the circumstances of its origin be not forgotten.

4. For the first forty years of their existence the Government notes, though always of growing importance, took a very minor place in the currency system of the country. This was partly due to an arrangement, now in gradual course of abolition, by which for the purposes of paper currency India has been divided up in effect into several separate countries. These

'circles,' as they are called, now seven[1] in number, correspond roughly to the principal provinces of India, the offices of issue being as follows :—

Calcutta	for	Bengal, Eastern Bengal, and Assam.
Cawnpore	„	the United Provinces.
Lahore	„	the Punjab and North-West Frontier Province.
Madras	„	the Madras Presidency and Coorg.
Bombay	„	Bombay and the Central Provinces.
Karachi	„	Sind.
Rangoon	„	Burma.

The currency notes[2] are in the form of promissory notes of the Government of India payable to the bearer on demand, and are of the denominations Rs. 5, 10, 50, 100, 500, 1000, and 10,000. Thus the lowest note is of the face value of 6s. 8d. They are issued without limit from any Paper Currency office in exchange for rupees or British gold coin, or (on the requisition of the Comptroller-General) for gold bullion.[3]

5. Up to 1910 the following arrangements were in force.

Every note was legal tender in its own circle. Payment of dues to the Government could be made in the currency notes of any circle; and railway companies could, if they accepted notes of any circle

[1] A rearrangement was made in 1910; previous to that date there were four circles and four sub-circles. It is no longer worth while to explain the relations which used to exist between the circles and sub-circles.

[2] For the legal provisions outlined in the following paragraphs see *Statistics of British India*, part iv. (a).

[3] For some further details see p. 9.

in payment of fares and freight, recover the value of them from the Government.

But, until recently, no notes were legal tender outside their own circle, and were payable only at the offices of issue of the town from which they were originally issued.

Beyond this the law imposed no obligation to pay. For the accommodation of the public, however, notes of other circles could be cashed at any Paper Currency office to such extent as the convenience of each office might permit. In ordinary circumstances every Government treasury, of which there are about 250, has cashed or exchanged notes if it could do so without inconvenience; and when this could not be done conveniently for large sums, small sums have generally been exchanged for travellers.

6. It is easy to understand the reasons for these restrictions. India is an enormously large country, over which the conditions of trade lead coins to ebb and flow within each year. At the beginning of the busy season when the autumn crops are harvested, rupees flow in great volume from the Presidency towns up country; in early spring they are carried to Burma for the rice crop; and so on—slowly finding their way back again to the Presidency towns during the summer. If the Government had made its notes encashable at a great variety of centres, it would have been taking on itself the expense and responsibility of carrying out these movements of

coin at different seasons of the year. When a country is habituated to the use of notes for making payments, they can be very usefully employed for purposes of remittance also. But a note-issuing authority puts itself in a difficulty if it provides facilities for remittance before a general habit has grown up of using notes for other purposes. If, on the other hand, the notes had been made universal legal tender, but only encashable at Presidency towns, there would undoubtedly have been a premium on coin at certain times of the year. And this would have greatly hindered the growth of the notes' popularity.

The Government, therefore, did what it could to make the notes useful and popular for purposes other than those of remittance; and it facilitated remittance so far as the proceeds of taxation, accumulating in its treasuries, permitted it to do this without expense. But it shrank from taking upon itself further responsibility. Its practice may be compared with that of the branches of the Reichsbank.

On the other hand, the objections to a policy, which divided the country up for the purposes of paper currency, are also plain. The limitation of the areas of legal tender and of the offices where the notes were encashable on demand greatly restricted the popularity of the notes. It might well have seemed worth while to popularise them, even at the expense of temporary loss. As soon as the public had become satisfied that the notes could be turned into coin readily and without question, their desire to cash them would probably have been greatly diminished. It is not certain that Government would have lost in the long-run if it had undertaken the responsibility and expense of regulating the flow of coin to the districts where it might be wanted at the different seasons of the year.

7. After the establishment of the Gold-Exchange Standard the importance of enlarging the functions of the note issue became apparent; and since 1900 the question of increasing the availability of the notes has been constantly to the front. In 1900 the Government issued a circular asking for opinions on certain proposals, including one for "universalising" the notes or making them legal tender in all circles. Some authorities thought that notes of small denominations (Rs. 5 and Rs. 10) might be safely universalised, without risk (on account of the trouble involved) of their being used for remittance on a large scale. It is on these lines that the use of the notes has been developed. In 1903 five-rupee notes were universalised except in Burma—that is to say, five-rupee notes of any circle were legal tender and encashable at any office of issue outside Burma; and in 1909 the Burmese limitation was removed.

In 1910 a great step forward was taken, and the law on the subject was consolidated by a new Act. Notes of Rs. 10 and Rs. 50 were universalised; and power was taken to universalise notes of higher denominations by executive order. In pursuance of this authority notes of Rs. 100 were universalised in 1911. "At the same time the receipt of notes of the higher denominations in circles other than the circle of issue, in payment of Government dues and in payments to railways, post and telegraph offices, was stopped by executive orders"; and "with a view to minimise any tendency to make use of the new universal notes for remittance purposes, it was decided concurrently with the new Act to offer facilities to bankers and merchants to make trade remittances between the currency centres by means of telegraphic orders granted by Government at a reduced rate of premium."[1] In the following year the Comptroller of Paper Currency reported that no difficulty whatever was experienced as the result of universalising the Rs. 10 and Rs. 50 notes; and the inconveniences, the fear of which had retarded the development of the note system for many years, were not realised.

8. The effect of these successive changes has been to make the old system of circles virtually inoperative. With notes of Rs. 100 universal legal tender it is difficult to see what can prevent the public from using them for purposes of remittance if they should wish to do so. The "circles" can no longer serve any useful purpose, and it would help to make clear

[1] Report of Comptroller of Paper Currency, 1910.

in the public mind the nature of the Indian note issue if they were to be abolished in name as well as in effect.

9. There must have been many occasions under the old system, on which ignorant persons suffered inconvenience through having notes of foreign circles passed off on them; and a long time may pass before distrust of the notes, as things not readily convertible, bred out of the memories of these occasions, entirely disappears. But, in combination with other circumstances, the universalising of the notes has had already a striking effect on the volume of their circulation, as is shown in the figures given below. It should be explained that by *gross* circulation (in the Government Statistics) is meant the value of all notes that have been issued and not yet paid off; that the *net* circulation is this sum less the value of notes held by Government in its own treasuries; and that the *active* circulation is the *net* reduced by the value of notes held by the Presidency banks at their head offices.[1] For some purposes the *active* circulation is the most important. But it is the reserve of rupees held against the *gross* circulation which is the best indication of the surplus volume of coined silver available, if necessary, for the purposes of circulation.

The following table gives for various years the

[1] Before 1893 these terms were used with a different significance. The statistics are still a little ambiguous as to whether for the net circulation the notes in Government reserve treasuries or the notes in *all* Government treasuries are to be deducted. I use the term in the latter sense.

average of the circulation on the last day of each month :—

	(In lakhs of rupees.)			(In £ million at 1s. 4d. the rupee throughout.)	
	Gross.	Net.	Active.	Gross.	Active.
1892–1893	2710	2333	1953	18	13
1893–1894	2829	2083	1785	19	12
1899–1900	2796	2367	2127	18½	14
1900–1901	2888	2473	2205	19½	14½
1902–1903	3374	2735	2349	22½	15½
1904–1905	3920	3276	2811	26	18½
1906–1907	4514	3949	3393	30	22½
1908–1909	4452	3902	3310	29½	22
1909–1910	4966	4535	3721	33	25
1910–1911	5435	4648	3875	36	26
1911–1912	5737	4949	4189	38	28

The following table gives in £ million the gross circulation of currency notes on March 31 of each year :—

	£ million.		£ million.
1900 . . .	19	1909 . . .	30½
1902 . . .	21	1910 . . .	36½
1904 . . .	25½	1911 . . .	36½
1906 . . .	30	1912 . . .	41
1908 . . .	31½	1913 . . .	46

The following table gives the average monthly gross circulation in £ million (at 1s. 4d. the rupee throughout) :—

	£ million.
Five years ending 1880–1881	8½
" " 1885–1886	9½
" " 1890–1891	11½
" " 1895–1896	19
" " 1900–1901	17½
" " 1905–1906	24
" " 1910–1911	32
The year 1911–1912	38

10. The rules governing the reserves which must be held against currency notes are very simple. A certain fixed maximum, the amount of which is determined from time to time by law, may be held invested, chiefly in Government of India rupee securities. Up to 1890 the invested portion of the reserve amounted to 600 lakhs (Rs. 600,00,000). This was increased to 700 lakhs in 1891, to 800 lakhs in 1892, to 1000 lakhs in 1897; to 1200 lakhs, of which 200 lakhs might be in English Government securities, in 1905; and to 1400 lakhs (£9,333,000), of which 400 lakhs (£2,666,000) might be in English securities, in 1911. The interest thus accruing on the invested portion of the reserve, less the expenses of the Paper Currency Department, is credited to the general revenues of the Government under the head "Profits of Note Circulation." This interest now amounts to £300,000 annually.

Up to 1898 the whole of the rest was held in silver coin in India. Under the Gold Note Act of 1898 the Government of India obtained authority to hold any part of the metallic portion of the reserve in gold coin. An Act of 1900 gave authority to hold part of this gold in London; but this power was only intended to be used for purposes of temporary convenience, and, although some gold was held in London in 1899 and 1900, this was not part of a permanent policy. An Act of 1905, however, gave full power to the Government to hold the metallic portion of the reserve, or any part of it, at its free discretion, either in London or in India, or partly in both places, and also in gold coin or bullion, or in rupees or silver bullion, subject only to the exception that all coined rupees should be kept in India and not in London. The actual figures, showing where the gold reserve has been held at certain dates, are given below.

GOLD IN PAPER CURRENCY RESERVE (£ MILLION).

March 31.	In India.	In London.	Total.
1897	nil	nil	nil
1898	¼	nil	¼
1899	2	nil	2
1900	7½	1½	9
1901	6	nil	6
1902	7	nil	7
1903	10	nil	10
1904	11	nil	11
1905	10½	nil	10½
1906	4	7	11
1907	3½	7	10½
1908	2½	3½	6
1909	nil	1½	1½
1910	6	2½	8½
1911	6	5	11
1912	15½	5½	21
1913	19½	6	25½

DISTRIBUTION OF RESERVE, MARCH 31, 1913.

Rupees	£11,000,000
Gold in India . . .	19,500,000
Gold in London . . .	6,000,000
Securities . . .	9,500,000
	£46,000,000

11. Gold was originally accumulated in the reserve in India through the automatic working of the rule by which rupees could be obtained in exchange for sovereigns. After exchange touched par in 1898, we see from the above table that gold began to flow in. When in 1900 the accumulations reached £5,000,000, attempts were made, in accordance with the recommendations of the Fowler Committee, to force it into circulation.[1] After the comparative failure of this attempt, and the passing of the Act of 1905, as described above, the Paper Currency Chest in England was instituted, and by 1906 about two-thirds of the gold which had been accumulated up to that time was transferred to this fund. This stock is kept at the Bank of England, but is not included in the Bank of England's own reserve. Gold which is thus transferred is said to be "ear-marked." The fund is under the absolute control of the Secretary of State for India in Council, and transferences to it are, so far as the accounts of the Bank of England are concerned, reckoned as exports. Policy as to how much of the gold should be kept in London and how much in India has fluctuated from time to time. I shall discuss it in Chapter VI.

12. These are the chief relevant facts of law. Important considerations of policy do not lie so plainly on the surface. Since 1899 the circulation of notes has more than doubled, but the invested

[1] For an account of this see p. 73.

portion of the reserve has been increased by only 40 per cent. As the note issue has become more firmly established and more widely used, a growing and not a diminishing proportion of the reserves has been kept in liquid form. This is due to a deliberate change of policy, and to the use of the liquid part of the reserve for a new purpose. The bullion reserve is no longer held solely with the object of securing the ability to meet the obligation to cash notes in legal tender (rupees or gold) on demand. It is now utilised for holding gold by means of which the Secretary of State can support exchange in times of depression and maintain at par the gold value of the rupee. For the sake of this object the Government are content to forgo the extra profit which might be gained by increasing the investments, and have steadily increased instead (as shown in the table on p. 49) the gold portion of the reserve. The Paper Currency Reserve is thus used to provide the gold which is the first line of defence of the currency system as a whole, and hence can hardly be distinguished from the resources of the Gold Standard Reserve proper.

It is not profitable to discuss the reserve policy of the Paper Currency under existing conditions in isolation from the other reserves which the Government now hold. The whole problem of the reserves, regarded as a current practical question, is dealt with in Chapter VI. In this chapter I wish to look at the matter from a broad standpoint, with an eye to the proper policy in a future, possibly remote.

13. The present policy was designed in its main outlines at a time when notes formed an insignificant part of the country's currency, and when the system of circles still greatly restricted their usefulness. The notes were at first, and were intended to be, little more than silver certificates. The rules governing the Reserve were framed (see § 3) at a time which, to the modern student of currency, is almost prehistoric, under the influence of the Bank of England's system of note issue and of the British Bank Act,—an Act which had the effect of destroying the importance of notes as a form of currency in England, and which it has been found impossible, in spite of some attempts, to imitate in the note-using countries of Europe. As has been urged in Chapter II., England is in matters of currency the worst possible model for India; for in no country are the conditions so wholly different. A good deal of experience with regard to note issues has now been accumulated elsewhere which ought some day to prove useful to India if her English rulers can sufficiently free themselves from their English traditions and preconceptions. Let me first give a short account of the nature of the seasonal demand for money in India; and then discuss the salient respects in which her system of note issue differs from those of typical note-using countries.

14. In contrast to what happens in the case of most note systems, the *gross* circulation in India diminishes instead of increasing during the busy seasons of autumn and spring. This is due to the fact that the Government Treasuries, the Presidency Banks, and possibly other banks and large merchants, use the notes as a convenient method of avoiding the custody of large quantities of silver during the slack season when rupees are not wanted.[1] That is to say, they deposit their surplus rupees during the summer in the Currency Reserve, holding their own reserves in the form of notes; and when the drain of rupees begins up country for moving the crops these notes have to be cashed. Thus in the dull season currency is largely in the hands of a class of persons and institutions which finds it most convenient to hold it in the form of notes, and in the busy season it is dissipated through the country and is, temporarily, in the hands of smaller men—cultivators who have sold their crops, small moneylenders and others, who habitually deal in small sums for which the rupee is the most convenient unit, or who do not yet understand the use of notes and still prefer, therefore, to be paid in actual coin.

15. Notes themselves, however, are used also, and to an increasing extent, for moving crops; and,

[1] At all times the vast bulk of the funds held by the Presidency Banks at their Head Offices is kept in notes, chiefly of high denominations (Rs. 1000 and Rs. 10,000); *e.g.* on December 31, 1911, £4,200,000 out of £4,800,000 was thus held.

although the *gross* circulation falls during the busy season for the reasons just given, the *active* circulation (*i.e.*, excluding the holdings of the Government Treasuries and the Presidency Banks) does, as we should expect, *increase* at this time of year. When, therefore, we are considering what proportion of liquid reserves ought to be maintained, or what part the note issue plays in supplying the much-needed element of elasticity in the busy season, it is of the active rather than of the gross circulation that we must take account. The figures are given below in lakhs of rupees :—

Months of Minimum and Maximum active circulation.	1906–1907.		1907–1908.[1]		1908–1909.		1909–1910.		1910–1911.		1911–1912.	
	1.	2.	1.	2.	1.	2.	1.	2.	1.	2.	1.	2.
Min.—												
June .	31,15	14,41	35,04	13,01	31.13	14,12	34,19	15,10	36,58	20,37	38,44	19,78
July .	32,43	12,87	34,43	15,89	31,58	16,52	34,31	17,22	36,56	22,60	39,15	21,14
August .	32,11	13,59	34,30	17,47	31,90	12,71	35,49	16,25	36,86	21,20	40,99	18,70
Max.—												
January .	35,54	9,11	33,20	8,62	33,67	8,54	41,47	10,37	39,67	11,45	44,14	10,56
Feb. .	36,07	9,42	33,28	9,38	34,36	9,50	41,45	9,12	40,95	12,57	44,58	12,61
March .	36,45	10,50	32,61	14,28	34,95	10,54	39,98	14,43	40,17	14,82	44,61	16,75

Columns (1): Active circulation. Columns (2): Holdings of Treasuries and Presidency Banks, *i.e.*, *excess* of gross over active circulation.

[1] An abnormal year.

We see, therefore, that, while the notes held by the Presidency Banks and the Treasury fall in the busy season by 700 to 1000 lakhs below their highest figure in the slack season, the *active* circulation *increases* in the busy season over its lowest figure in the slack season by about 400 lakhs (in the latest year for which we have figures, 1911–1912, by more than

600 lakhs). Of course this is not a very high proportion of the total increase in the volume of currency which is required in the busy season. But it is an amount well worth considering, and these figures put the note issue in a more favourable light as a source of currency in the busy season than is usually realised. The relative importance of notes and rupees[1] in supplying the seasonal needs of trade is well shown in the following table:—

NET ABSORPTION (IN LAKHS OF RUPEES) OF CURRENCY INTO CIRCULATION (+) OR RETURN OF CURRENCY FROM CIRCULATION (−).[1]

Year.	April to June.		July to Sept.		Oct. to Dec.		Jan. to March.		Whole Year.	
	Rupees.	Notes.	Rupees.	Notes.	Rupees.	Notes.	Rupees.	Notes.	Rupees.	Notes.
1905–1906	−116	+ 83	+339	+ 58	+1139	+175	+ 88	+101	+1450	+417
1906–1907	− 24	−148	+600	+220	+1068	+310	+156	0	+1800	+382
1907–1908	+182	−141	+145	+ 29	+ 735	−126	−670	−146	+ 392	−384
1908–1909	−798	−148	−718	+198	+ 339	+112	−311	+ 72	−1488	+234
1909–1910	+ 47	− 76	− 58	+286	+1065	+130	+268	+163	+1322	+503
1910–1911	−287	−340	−100	+147	+ 722	+144	− 1	+ 68	+ 334	+ 19
1911–1912	−130	−173	+220	+262	+ 499	+356	+565	− 1	+1154	+444

1 In this table rupees (but not notes) in the Presidency Banks are treated as being in circulation. It would be a troublesome piece of work to exclude them, and would make, I think, very little difference to the result. The main variable element in the reserves of the Presidency Banks is the notes, and these are duly allowed for in the above table.

The above table is exceedingly instructive. It shows that the notes supply an increasingly important proportion of the seasonal demand for additional currency. It shows also that the demand for notes from one year to another has been of a steadier character than the demand for rupees. In the period

1 The part played by gold is discussed in Chapter IV.

of depression from the winter of 1907 until the autumn of 1908 the active rupee circulation was much harder hit than the active note circulation; for in the six months January to June 1908 the rupee circulation fell by 1468 lakhs, while the active note circulation fell by 294 lakhs, and for the nine months January to September 1908 the former fell by 2186 lakhs, while the latter fell by only 96 lakhs.[1]

16. Let me now turn to three salient characteristics, all closely connected with one another, and chiefly distinguishing the Indian system of paper currency from those of most note-using countries.

In the first place, the function of note issue is wholly dissociated in India from the function of banking. To discount bills is one of the functions of banks. Where there are Central Banks with the right of note issue, they are usually able, subject to various restrictions, to increase their note issue at certain seasons of the year in order to discount more bills.

In the second place, as there is no Central Bank in India, there is no Government Banker. It is true that the Government keep some funds (rather more than £2,000,000, as a rule) at the three Presidency Banks. But the bulk of their floating resources is held either in London or in cash in their own Treasuries in India. Thus, as in the United States, the Government maintains an independent Treasury system. This

[1] I estimate that at this date the total volume of the active rupee circulation was between five and six times the total volume of the active note circulation.

means, just as it does in the United States, that, at certain seasons of the year when taxes are flowing in fastest, funds may sometimes be withdrawn from the money market. The difficulty and inconvenience to which this system has given rise in the United States are well known to those who are acquainted with the recent financial history of that country. The ill effects of it are to a certain extent counteracted, in the case of India, by a transference of these funds to London and a release of the accumulating currency in India through the sale of Council Bills. But this is not a perfect solution.

The third and most important point arises out of the first two. The Indian currency is internally (*i.e.*, apart from the import of funds from foreign countries) absolutely inelastic. There is no method whatever by which the volume of currency can be *temporarily* expanded by some credit device *within* the country to meet the regularly recurrent seasonal demands of trade. Cheque-using countries meet the difficulty by increasing the volume of credit created by the banks; most note-using countries meet it by the Central Bank's discounting a greater volume of home bills than usual, and thus increasing its note circulation temporarily, without a corresponding increase in its metallic reserves. Except for a certain proportion of the business which is transacted by cheque (chiefly in the Presidency towns), there is nothing corresponding to this in India.

Additional currency, whether notes or rupees, can be obtained in two ways only — by buying Council Bills in London or by bringing in sovereigns. Additional notes or rupees can be obtained in payment of Council Bills or in exchange for sovereigns, but not otherwise. The fact that a temporary increase in the media of exchange can only be obtained by bringing in funds from abroad partly explains the high rate of discount in India during the busy season. This question will be more fully dealt with in Chapter VIII. But the main point can be put briefly thus :—If funds are to be attracted from abroad for a short period (say three months), the rate of interest must be high enough to repay the cost of remittance *both* ways, which in the case of places so remote from one another as India and London is considerable. If there were some authority which could create credit money in India during the busy season, it would not be necessary for the rate of discount to rise so high.

17. The objections to the existing arrangements largely arise, therefore, out of the absence of a State Bank. This question is further discussed in Chapters VI. and VII. I feel little doubt that India ought to have a State Bank, associated in a greater or less degree with the Government. The Government is drifting year by year into doing more business of an essentially banking character; and as time goes on it will become increasingly objectionable

to dissociate some of the functions of modern State Banking from others. But there is a considerable weight of opinion in favour of the view that the time for the establishment of a Central Indian Bank is not yet ripe. In the meantime is any partial remedy possible for the evils dealt with above?

18. I am inclined to think that such a remedy is possible. The manner in which the reserve against the note issue must be kept is needlessly restricted. Apart from that portion which is permanently invested, the whole must be kept in gold and silver. This is in imitation of the rules governing the Bank of England's note issue. But the note-issuing banks of Europe afford a better model. It might be proper to prescribe by law the holding of a certain proportion of the reserve (say one-third[1]) in gold or silver coin. A further amount might be held, as at present, permanently invested in Government of India securities. With regard to the rest the Government should, I think, permit itself much greater latitude. It should be free to lend it out on suitable security, either in India or London, for periods not exceeding three months. In London it should be lent out on the same conditions as the Cash Balances and the Gold-Exchange Standard (see Chapter VI.) are lent out at present. To lend in London would be technically convenient (for the reasons given on

[1] The proper proportion would partly depend upon the policy pursued in regard to the Gold Standard Reserve.

p. 172), but it would not cure the inelasticity of the Indian system. Part of the reserve should, therefore, be lent out *in India*. Suitable security for this purpose would be Government of India securities (which would have indirectly the effect of increasing the market for Rupee Paper) and Bills of Exchange of the highest class. It is not worth while to discuss here in detail the precise methods which it would be proper for the Government to adopt in lending out funds in India either from the Cash Balances or from the Paper Currency Reserve. Whether it were done through the Presidency Banks only, or whether an approved list of borrowers of Government funds were to be drawn up for India as is already the case for London, the effect on the Indian Money Market would be much the same. The needed element of elasticity would be obtained, and the present absolute dependence of India on London for an expansion of currency would be modified. I shall return to this proposal again in Chapters VI. and VIII. Its full force cannot be shown until we have discussed the question of the Secretary of State's reserves as a whole, and have studied in detail the movements of the Indian bank rate.

A good deal of opinion has been expressed in India lately in favour of loans being made there from the Government's Cash Balances. In so far as this opinion demands some new machinery by which on suitable occasions the Government can lend out funds in India herself, the evil which it seeks to remedy is a real one. And the method proposed above is, I believe, the right way in which to approach the problem's solution.

19. The discussion of this question will be concluded in Chapters VI., VII., and VIII. But it will be well to say a few words at once with a view to avoiding misunderstandings on two points. It has been necessary in the immediate past to use the Paper Currency Reserve as a part of the general reserves held for ensuring the absolute stability of the rupee. I do not advocate the lending out in India of any part of this reserve, or of the Cash Balances, at the expense of the stability of the Gold Standard, or until adequate measures can be taken in other ways to ensure this. But I think the time has practically arrived when the whole of the liquid portion of the Paper Currency Reserve is not required, in addition to the Gold Standard Reserve proper, for this purpose. A busy season will soon come when the Government might lend some part of its reserves in India without endangering in the least the stability of its system and to the great advantage of Indian trade. It ought, at least, to have the power to do this.

20. The remaining point is this. A provision of the above kind for introducing some degree of elasticity into the Indian currency system would not be very useful in a season such as that of the autumn and winter of 1905–6 or of the autumn of 1912–13, when there was a demand for rupees on so great a scale

that it could only be met from the Mint. Additions to the currency of this kind can only be made by importing funds from abroad. But these are permanent not temporary additions. Every such addition makes a similar demand for new coinage in succeeding seasons less likely. They are abnormal, and recent history seems to show that these permanent additions to the Indian currency are not made by slow and steady accretions year by year, but in great bursts of activity at considerable intervals. In years of normal activity, therefore, there may be considerable stores of rupees lying idle in the reserves beyond what is required for the safety of the currency. Indian bankers and merchants can only get at these rupees, so as to obtain a net addition to the currency, by buying sovereigns or Council Bills in London. If the use for the additional currency is only temporary, the cost of transport or remittance is great enough to make it not worth their while to get this addition until the Indian rate of discount has been forced up to a high level. If the Government were free on such occasions to lend out some part of the rupees, against high-class security, at 5 or even 6 per cent, this would be profitable to the Government, and would prevent the discount rate from reaching a level which is caused, not by anxiety, but merely by the expense arising out of the distance between London and Calcutta.

CHAPTER IV

THE PRESENT POSITION OF GOLD IN INDIA AND PROPOSALS FOR A GOLD CURRENCY

1. THE Fowler Committee of 1898 avowed themselves in favour of the ultimate establishment of a gold *currency* in India as well as a gold *standard*. Paragraph 54 of their Report runs as follows :—

> We are in favour of making the British sovereign a legal tender and a current coin in India. We also consider that, at the same time, the Indian mints should be thrown open to the unrestricted coinage of gold on terms and conditions such as govern the three Australian branches of the Royal Mint. The result would be that, under dentical conditions, the sovereign would be coined and would circulate both at home and in India. Looking forward as we do to the effective establishment in India of a gold standard and currency based on the principles of the free in-flow and out-flow of gold, we recommend these measures for adoption.

The first part of their proposal was carried out immediately, and, in 1899, British gold was declared legal tender at the rate of a sovereign to 15 rupees. It appeared at first as if their further object of a gold currency might soon be attained also. The principle of minting gold in India was accepted both by the Secretary of State and by the Viceroy's Council, and in 1900 Sir Clinton Dawkins actually announced that it had been decided to constitute a branch of the Mint at Bombay for this purpose. In the meantime an attempt was made, described in § 4, to force sovereigns into circulation. But the attempt failed, and Sir Clinton Dawkins's proposal was never carried out. As Sir G. Fleetwood Wilson explained in the Legislative Council in 1911—

> A number of technical and other difficulties were raised by the Royal Mint, which ultimately wore out the patience of Lord Curzon's Government. In the interval the Kolar gold mining companies had mostly entered into agreements for the sale of their produce in England; and the prospect of their bringing their gold to be refined and coined at Bombay —which was to be the *pièce de résistance* of our gold mint —was thus deferred. In the circumstances it was decided in 1902 to drop the project, and to wait until a stronger demand for a local gold coinage should arise.

This account of the matter, however, scarcely does justice to the part played by the British Treasury in defeating the project. The official correspondence, lately published,[1] shows that for two years (from 1899 to 1901) they made, as Sir G. F. Wilson states, a succession of technical difficulties in a spirit of scarcely veiled hostility to the whole proposal. But eventually (in May 1901) a scheme was arranged, acceptable both to the Mint at home and to the

[1] H. of C. 495 of 1913.

authorities in India. At this point in the negotiations the natural instincts of the Treasury officials became uncontrollable, and respect for the independence of the India Office had to be abandoned. Their first line of defence in the form of technical difficulties having been overcome, they fell back upon open argument as to the wisdom from the Indian point of view of the whole project:—

> While expressing their satisfaction that an agreement has now been reached, my Lords think it desirable, before practical steps are taken to carry out the scheme, to invite Lord George Hamilton to review the arguments originally advanced in favour of the coinage of the sovereign in India, and to consider whether the course of events, in the two years which have elapsed since the proposal was made, has not tended to diminish their force, and to render such advantages as are likely to accrue from the establishment of a branch mint wholly incommensurate with the expense to be incurred. . . . The gold standard is now firmly established, and the public requires no proof of the intention of the Indian Government not to go back on their policy, which is beyond controversy. Sovereigns are readily attracted to India when required under existing conditions. . . . On the other hand, the estimates of the Government of India of gold available for coinage in that country are less than was anticipated, nor is any considerable increase expected, at any rate for some time. . . . The staff would have to be maintained in idleness for a large part of the year at considerable cost to the Indian Exchequer. . . . It is of course for Lord George Hamilton to decide whether, in spite of these objections, the scheme is to be proceeded with.

The India Office answered thus:—

> The establishment of a mint for the coinage of gold in India is the clearest outward sign that can be given of the consummation of the new currency system; and to abandon the proposal now must attract attention and provoke criticism and unrest. . . . His Lordship is not inclined to abandon the scheme at the stage which it has now reached.

The Treasury's reply was cogent:—

> My Lords cannot believe that the position of the gold standard in India will be strengthened, or public confidence in the intentions of the Government confirmed, by providing machinery for obtaining gold coins which is neither demanded nor required by the mercantile community; while, on the other hand, the failure or only partial success of a gold mint would undoubtedly be pointed to by the opponents of the gold standard policy (although without justification) as evidence of the breakdown of that policy.

The Treasury's arguments were, as they deserved to be, successful. After consultation with the Government of India, who drew attention to the agreements (referred to by Sir G. F. Wilson above) entered into by the mining companies, the Secretary of State agreed (Feb. 6, 1903) to the project's indefinite postponement. "No public explanation was given in India of this sudden recession from what has hitherto been regarded as an essential feature of the currency policy inaugurated in 1893 and definitely established on the recommendations of the Currency Committee of 1898."[1]

2. From 1903 up to 1910 little was heard of pro-

[1] This quotation is from a letter addressed by the Government of India to the Secretary of State, nine years later (May 16, 1912).

posals for an active encouragement of the circulation of gold. But the intention had never been repudiated, and in the Budget debate of 1910 Sir James Meston, then Financial Secretary to the Government, spoke as follows :—

> The broad lines of our action and our objects are clear and unmistakable, and there has been no great or fundamental sacrifice of consistency in progress towards our ideal. Since the Fowler Commission that progress has been real and unbroken. There is still one great step forward before the ideal can be reached. We have linked India with the gold countries of the world, we have reached a gold-exchange standard, which we are steadily developing and improving. The next and final step is a true gold currency. That, I have every hope, will come in time, but we cannot force it. The backwardness of our banking arrangements, the habits and suspicions of the people, the infancy of co-operation—all stand in the way. But the final step will come when the country is ripe for it. I trust that will not long be delayed; for when it comes, it will obliterate all the mistakes, all the inconveniences, all the artificialities, of our present position.

In March 1911 matters were carried a step further, Sir Guy Fleetwood Wilson replying in the Legislative Council to Sir Vithaldas Thackersey (who had argued that a 10-rupee gold coin ought to be minted and put into active circulation in India) that "much has happened since 1902 which justifies the reopening of the question." In a despatch to the Secretary of State, dated May 16, 1912, the Government of India proposed to open the Bombay Mint to the coinage of sovereigns. This is an exceedingly confused document. It is mainly directed to showing that an increased use of gold as currency in India would be advantageous to the system. But, apart from the validity of this argument, it is not clearly shown in what way the establishment of a mint would effect the desired purpose; indeed it is explicitly admitted that "in proposing to open a gold mint it is not our intention to induce thereby an increased flow of gold to India. Indeed were that our purpose we recognise that it would certainly fail." The despatch reads as though it were an attempt to reconcile divergent and contradictory views which had received expression. The British Treasury, however, has again come to the rescue. They have stipulated either that the branch mint should be under Imperial management, which would be inconvenient, or that it should be wholly separate, which would be expensive. Accordingly, in a despatch, dated October 18, 1912, the Secretary of State suggested to the Government of India that instead of sovereigns Indian gold coins of the denomination of, say, 10 rupees should be coined at Bombay. The Government of India have replied that they prefer this proposal to the conditions demanded by the Treasury, and that they contemplate making inquiries as to Indian opinion on it. This is how the matter stands at present.

The actual policy of the Government of India since 1900 as regards gold currency has been, in my opinion, well judged. But these negotiations show that the authorities are still doubtful as to the advantages of the existing system.

3. Up to 1870 the English currency system was the envy of the rest of the world, and it was supposed that the excellencies of the practical working of this system were due to the fact that the actual circulating medium of the country was gold. This, it was thought, must be the only really safe way of maintaining absolute stability. Germany, accordingly, when she instituted her gold standard, prohibited the issue of notes of a less denomination than 100 marks, in order that gold might actually circulate from hand to hand to a maximum possible amount. For similar reasons the business community showed themselves immovably hostile to Lord Goschen's proposals for the issue of one-pound notes in England. While other countries, who have, with few exceptions, found the expense of a gold medium of exchange prohibitively heavy, have nevertheless envied those who could afford it, and have adapted their laws, even when they could not afford to adapt their practice, to a currency of gold.

But in recent years the evolution of currency has, for reasons which I have elaborated in Chapter II., embarked upon a new stage of development, and all this is changed. In England the use of a cheque currency has grown so universal that the composition of the metallic coin has become a matter of secondary importance. In Germany the policy of 1876 has been deliberately reversed by a recent revision of the Bank Act, and 20-mark notes are now issued with the deliberate object of keeping as much gold as possible in the bank and wasting as little as possible in circulation. This new policy is likely to be extended in the future. The President of the Reichsbank, addressing the Budget Committee of the Reichstag in January 1913, argued that the rule laid down in 1906, forbidding the free issue of 20- and 50-mark notes to an amount exceeding £15,000,000, would have to be repealed, the issue of these notes in 1912 having exceeded the limit by £11,500,000; and he went on to say that they must, in the interests of sound policy, increase the issue of notes and thus hold a larger quantity of gold in their reserves.

In other countries, where actual currency is the principal medium of exchange, the attempt to introduce gold as the medium passing from hand to hand has been for the most part abandoned. A great part of the new gold has flowed, during the last ten years, into the reserves of the State Banks, and a comparatively small amount only can have found its way into circulation. In Austria-Hungary, for example, after the currency reform of 1892, attempts were made to force gold into circulation just as they were in India. They luckily failed. The authorities of the Austro-Hungarian Bank now keep all the gold they can in their central reserves, and they are not likely to make another attempt to dissipate it. The same kind of thing occurred in Russia. After establishing with difficulty a gold standard, they began with the theory, and have since abandoned it, that a gold currency was the natural corollary. Other examples could be given. A gold standard is the rule now in all parts of the world; but a gold currency is the exception. The "sound currency" maxims of twenty or thirty years ago are still often repeated, but they have not been successful, nor ought they to have been, in actually influencing affairs. I think I am right in saying that Egypt is now the only country in the world in which actual gold coins are the principal medium of exchange.[1]

The reasons for this change are easily seen. It has been found that the expense of a gold circulation is insupportable, and that large economies can be safely effected by the use of some cheaper substitute; and it has been found further that gold in the pockets of the people is not in the least available at a time of crisis or to meet a foreign drain. For these purposes the gold resources of a country must be centralised.

[1] The value of the token coins (silver, nickel, and bronze) circulating in Egypt and the Sudan is estimated at no more than £E3,600,000, and the notes of the National Bank of Egypt (chiefly current in the large towns) at £E2,400,000. The whole of the rest of the currency consists of gold coins (chiefly British sovereigns). The existing position in Egypt is, therefore, the ideal at which many Indian currency reformers seem to aim.

This view has long been maintained by economists.[1] Ricardo's proposals for a sound and economical currency were based on the principle of keeping gold out of actual circulation. Mill (*Political Economy*, Bk. III. chap. xxii. § 2) argued that "gold wanted for exportation is almost invariably drawn from the reserves of banks, and is never likely to be taken from the outside circulation while the banks remain solvent." While Goschen spoke as follows in 1891 before the London Chamber of Commerce :—

> We only have as an effective circulation that which is required for the daily wants of the people. You cannot tap that to any extent so as to increase your central stock of gold. You may raise your rate of interest to 6 per cent or 8 per cent, but the bulk of the people will not carry less gold in their pockets than they did before, and I doubt whether, from other quarters, you would be able to get much addition to your central store.

But while it is no new theory that gold in the pockets of the people is absolutely useless for the purposes for which a currency reserve is held, all but the highest authorities have believed until fairly recently that no gold standard can be really stable, unless gold actually circulates in the country. The contrary view was distrusted by practical financiers, and only of late years has it become powerful enough to dictate policies. At last, however, Governments have been converted to it, and it is now as much

[1] See Lindsay's evidence before Indian Currency Committee (1898), Q. 3404.

their anxiety to keep gold out of circulation and in their reserves as it was formerly the opposite.

A preference for a tangible gold currency is no longer more than a relic of a time when Governments were less trustworthy in these matters than they are now, and when it was the fashion to imitate uncritically the system which had been established in England and had seemed to work so well during the second quarter of the nineteenth century.

4. Let us now apply these general considerations to the case of India. In 1900 an attempt was seriously made to get sovereigns into active circulation, in accordance with the recommendations of the Committee of 1898. It was decided to pay out gold to the public as soon as the stock should exceed five millions sterling, and such payments commenced on January 12, 1900, at the currency offices in Calcutta, Madras, and Bombay. The instructions issued were to tender gold to all presenters of notes, but to give rupees if they were preferred. Later on the Comptroller-General was authorised to send sovereigns to the larger district treasuries. And in March the Post Offices in the Presidency towns began to give gold in payment of money orders, and the Presidency Banks were requested to issue sovereigns in making payments on Government account. These arrangements continued in force throughout the financial year 1900–1901, and by March 31, 1901, the amount put into the hands of the public

reached the considerable total of £6,750,000. But of this amount part was exported, not far short of half was returned to Government, and it was supposed that the greater part of the remainder went into the hands of bullion dealers.[1] Further attempts to force gold into circulation were, therefore, abandoned, and a large part of the gold which had accumulated in the currency reserve in India was, a little later on, shipped to England in order to be held "ear-marked" at the Bank of England

Since that time the provisions of the Indian system regarding gold (as already given in Chapter I.) have been as follows:—(1) The sovereign is legal tender in India at 15 rupees to £1; (2) the Government has bound itself by Notification to give rupees for sovereigns at this rate; (3) it is willing, as a rule, to give sovereigns for rupees at this rate, but is under no legal obligation to do so, and will not always exchange large quantities.

5. The defeat of the experiment of 1900–1901 was due to a variety of causes, but mainly, I should suppose, to the long habituation of the Indian public to the use of silver, and to the unsuitability of the sovereign, by reason of its high value, for so poor a country as India.

But it is not by any means so certain that an attempt at the present time to put a 10-rupee gold

[1] The above account is summarised from the Reports of the Comptroller of Paper Currency for 1900 and 1901.

coin into circulation would not meet with more success. Its value would be somewhat less. But, more important than this, the taste of India for gold, as against silver, has been very considerably developed during the last ten years. It will be worth while to summarise the available evidence as to the present position of gold in India.

6. We know, of course, what the annual net addition to the total stock of gold in India (*i.e.*, the imports and the production less the exports) approximately is—although the amount of the steady leakage across the land frontiers is usually neglected.[1] We know also how much of this addition is in the form of sovereigns, and how much in the form of gold bars. By making allowance, therefore, for the increase or decrease of sovereigns in the Paper Currency Reserve and the Government Treasuries, we can calculate how many sovereigns have found their way each year into the hands of the public. But as to the uses to which the public put the sovereigns our information is exceedingly vague and unprecise. By far the most careful and valuable discussions of the question are to be found in the Reports of the Comptroller-General of

[1] This is probably very considerable. India must be the main source of supply of gold for the whole of Central Asia. The following extract from a report sent in to the Comptroller of Currency (1911–12) is instructive:—"From Peshawar a considerable absorption of gold in connection with the trans-border trade is reported; this trade is said to have amounted during 1911–12 to the value of Rs. 30 lakhs. Gold so taken seldom or never returns. The Amir's subsidy is also largely paid in gold." It is also reported that gold is preferred by those who go on pilgrimage to Mecca.

Paper Currency for 1910–11 (written by Mr. R. W. Gillan) and for 1911–12 (written by Mr. M. F. Gauntlett); and I have made free use of these in what follows. First, it will be useful to have before us the statistical information referred to above:—

	(1)=(2)+(3) Net Addition to Stock of Gold:— Imports – Exports + Production.	(2) Net Addition to Gold in Paper Currency Reserve and Treasuries.[1]	(3)=(4)+(5) Net Addition to Stock of Gold in Hands of Public.	(4) Net Addition to Bullion in Hands of Public.	(5) Net Addition to Sovereigns in Hands of Public.
	£	£	£	£	£
1901–02	3,223,000	– 5,000	3,228,000	2,261,000	967,000
1902–03	7,882,000	2,870,000	5,012,000	2,814,000	2,198,000
1903–04	8,963,000	944,000	8,019,000	4,741,000	3,278,000
1904–05	8,841,000	38,000	8,803,000	5,866,000	2,937,000
1905–06	2,698,000	– 6,840,000	9,538,000	5,806,000	3,732,000
1906–07	12,061,000	– 193,000	12,254,000	7,098,000	5,156,000
1907–08	13,677,000	– 993,000	14,670,000	7,243,000	7,427,000
1908–09	5,022,000	– 2,843,000	7,865,000	4,422,000	3,443,000
1909–10	16,620,000	6,347,000	10,273,000	7,407,000	2,866,000
1910–11	18,153,000	71,000	18,082,000	9,991,000	8,091,000
1911–12	27,345,000	9,347,000	17,998,000	9,117,000	8,881,000
1912–13[2]	24,551,000	4,231,000	20,320,000	9,320,000	11,000,000

[1] Since 1908 the whole of this has been held in sovereigns.
[2] Estimate.

7. The enormous amount of wealth which the Indian people are now devoting to the barren accumulation of gold is brought out very strikingly by the figures in the third column. We know that it is hoarded, used as jewellery, as gilding, even (according to Messrs. Samuel Montagu) as medicine. But these figures are not relevant to our present purpose, and we must turn to the figures in the last column, giving the flow of sovereigns into the hands of the public. What part of this total is employed for ornament,

what part for hoarding, what part is melted down, and what part is left truly to serve as currency?

In the first place it is estimated that about £1,000,000 "shield" sovereigns are now imported annually. These are sought after for purposes of ornament and stand at a premium.[1] It may be safely assumed, therefore, that they are not used as currency. Further, it is certain that a large number are melted every year and used as bullion. There are two causes of this. "As regards melting," writes Mr. Gillan,[2] "it is to be noted that for certain purposes the sovereign has at all times an advantage. Gold being sold in 5- and 10-ounce bars, if a jeweller wants only a small quantity, a full-weight sovereign meets his purpose very well, as he knows its exact weight, fineness, and value, and has no trouble in obtaining it. And the sovereign is presumably cheaper than the same quantity of gold in out-of-the-way parts." There is also another cause, connected with the exchanges;[3] at some times of year the cheapest way of getting gold is to buy sovereigns for rupees from the Government. This explanation is borne out by the fact that there is a steady demand for sovereigns from the Government's reserves during the summer months. This is the time when the exchanges make it most advantageous to get gold in this way, and when there is least likely to be a demand for sovereigns as a

1 Throughout 1911-12 the Bank of Bengal quoted them at a premium of 4d.

2 Report on Paper Currency, 1911-12.

3 See pp. 97-99.

medium of exchange. Many sovereigns, therefore, are melted. But we should be making rather a random guess if we were to attempt to say how many.

There must still remain, as the result of recent importations, a large number of sovereigns retained in the hands of the public in that form. But we cannot assume that even this reduced total is truly employed as a medium of exchange. There is a good deal of evidence for supposing that in some parts of the country sovereigns are displacing rupees for the purpose of hoards. This may be the case even when in the first instance the gold is used for currency. The crops may be sold for gold, because the cultivator wants gold for his hoard. "It is quite conceivable," Mr. Gillan points out, "that the acceptance by the cultivator of gold in payment of his crops is in the nature of barter; that is to say, he takes the gold not as coin merely but for some other purpose, and the return of gold in payment of revenue may be no more than the return of so much as he finds himself unable to retain."

8. It is clear, then, that we must not fly from a glance at column (1) of the table on p. 76, or even from a glance at column (5), to extravagant conclusions as to the present position of the sovereign in the Indian currency system. Many heavy deductions must be made from the first totals. What direct evidence is there as to the use of gold as currency?

"The best indication" (to quote Mr. Gillan again)

"of the extent to which sovereigns have established themselves as a regular part of the currency, is to be found in the figures of receipts at Post Offices and Railways." These have been as follows :—

	Post Offices.	Railways.
1906–07	£553,000 [1]	£468,000 [1]
1907–08	1,358,000	1,045,000
1908–09	1,001,000	710,000
1909–10	265,000	134,000
1910–11	638,000	597,000
1911–12	1,363,000	1,222,000

[1] Second half-year only.

It has been estimated by the Paper Currency Department [1] that in 1907, as a result of the absorption of earlier years, not less than two millions were in circulation. But it is supposed that by the end of 1908 nearly the whole of that amount had disappeared. Owing to the depression of that year and the low level of the exchanges, the most profitable employment of the sovereigns was as bullion. This is strikingly borne out by the almost negligible receipts of gold (given below) by Post Offices and Railways in 1909–10. Until 1910 the absorption of sovereigns was not sufficient to restore them to a position of any importance as currency. We have chiefly to consider, therefore, the imports of sovereigns since 1910. It is from this source that the sovereigns now circulating as currency are likely to have come.

[1] See Report for 1909.

9. When we proceed to detail, it appears that there are several important parts of India in which the use of the sovereign is still negligible—in Bengal, Eastern Bengal, Assam, the Central Provinces, and Burma. In these provinces it has not begun to make any serious headway. In the United Provinces (for the purchase of wheat) and in certain districts of Madras, on the other hand, sovereigns seem to circulate to some extent, to be received freely by the general public, and to be increasing, though at no sensational rate. In Bombay and the Punjab, particularly in the latter, their use is, however, much more important. Most of the detailed evidence, which is available, refers to the Punjab; and care must be taken not to apply to the whole of India opinions from witnesses in that province as to the present position of gold. The following extract from a resolution passed by the Punjab Chamber of Commerce on June 4, 1912, is interesting. The Chamber "are able to state authoritatively that sovereigns are becoming popular and that their circulation is increasing. They are accepted as legal tender in the bazaars, and this may be attributed to the intelligence of the people and to the fact that all over the East (in China and the Straits Settlements), where the Punjab Sepoys serve in the army and the police, the sovereign is popular. These men remit their earnings in gold, and as there is hardly a village in the Punjab that has not sent a man to these services, it is not sur-

prising that the value of the sovereign is understood. It is difficult to say to what extent sovereigns are being hoarded, but that they are held up by the well-to-do to a very considerable amount is undoubtedly the case; and hoarding will continue among the rural population for years to come. With regard to the probable effect this importation of sovereigns may have on exchange, they are of opinion that Government should not rely on the sovereigns that are being absorbed by the districts in exchange for produce and in the shape of savings coming out at any time in any appreciable quantity to support the stability of the rupee." In 1911–12 the Comptroller of Currency collected a number of district reports as to the growing popularity of gold in the Punjab. They completely corroborate the above summary.

10. Before we pass on to other aspects of the question, a word may be added with special reference to the very large gold imports of quite recent date (*i.e.*, in 1912). Popular attention has been attracted by the figures for that year, which are indeed truly remarkable.[1] The gold imports of 1911–12 and 1912–13 (see table on p. 76) were noteworthy as compared with those of former years by reason of their huge aggregate amount; but they were even more noteworthy if regard be had to the very high proportion of sovereigns.

[1] In the *calendar* year 1912 India increased her stock of gold by £29,500,000, of which about £21,500,000 was in sovereigns.

I do not believe, however, that a conclusion can fairly be drawn from these figures as to any startling change in the position of the sovereign in India. India has experienced two very good seasons and has been able, therefore, to accumulate savings to an unusually large extent for investment in gold ornaments and hoards. Is this altogether inadequate as a partial explanation of the recorded figures? I do not, for the following reasons, think it is.

In the first place the gold imports for 1911–12 fall short of, and those for 1912–13 do not much exceed, those for 1910–11 if we exclude the additions to the Paper Currency Reserve. Imports of gold for this purpose are, for reasons to be explained in Chapter V., quite independent of the effective desire of India for gold, and occur merely because gold happens in some circumstances to be a cheaper means of remittance to India than Council Bills or any other method. In the second place the conditions of 1912 were somewhat abnormal on account of the unusually large supplies of gold which were available from Australia and Egypt If it is a matter of importing gold from England, those who want it for bullion purposes will generally find it cheaper to buy gold bars than to buy gold coin. But if there are sovereigns on their way from Australia and ready to be diverted to India, or if there are surplus sovereigns available for export at Alexandria, it may be a good deal cheaper to buy these sovereigns than to get gold bars from London. The explanation of this, depending on the foreign exchanges, is fully discussed in Chapter V. I suspect, therefore, that a higher proportion than usual of the sovereigns imported in 1912 were put to non-currency uses for which gold bars would have served just as well. If sovereigns rather than bars are imported *from London* it is reasonable to draw the conclusion that the importer (since he must pay a higher price) definitely prefers them. But if sovereigns are imported from Egypt or Australia rather than bars from London, no such conclusion can be drawn. Of the 21,500,000 sovereigns imported into India in 1912 only about 5,000,000 came from London—the rest from Egypt and Australia.[1] From the gross figures of gold imports into India in 1912 even heavier deductions than usual must be made, therefore, before we have an indication of the extent to which additional sovereigns have really found their way into the currency.[2]

[1] The fluctuations in the proportions for different years of the figures in columns (4) and (5) of the table on p. 76 must certainly be explained in part by the state of the exchanges, and not wholly by the degree of deliberate preference for sovereigns.

[2] The Accountant-General, Bombay, has suggested (*see* Paper Currency Report, 1911–1912) that "the principal cause" of the heavy importation of sovereigns has been a reduction in the rate of charge (from $\frac{1}{16}$ per cent to $\frac{1}{32}$ per cent) for Telegraphic Transfers issued upon Madras and Calcutta against gold imported into Bombay. No doubt, this favours gold to a slightly greater extent than before, as against Council Transfers, as a means of remittance from London to Madras and Calcutta, but the difference seems too small in relation to the other factors which determine the cheapest form of remittance, for the change to have exerted any appreciable influence.

11. Perhaps we may fairly sum this evidence up by saying that it goes to show the existence in India at the present time of an enormous demand for gold bullion, a very considerable demand for sovereigns for purposes of hoarding, and a relatively smaller demand for them, chiefly confined to the United Provinces, the Punjab, Madras, and Bombay, for purposes of currency.

Those who think that this tendency to use gold coins should be further encouraged have advocated three methods of doing so: by making arrangements for the coinage of sovereigns at Bombay; by the mintage there of some distinctively Indian coin of the denomination of 10 rupees; by a deliberate attempt on the part of Government, as in 1900–1901, to force sovereigns into circulation and to familiarise parts of the country with them where they are at present unfamiliar, even to the extent of refusing to issue more rupees on demand.

12. I have placed these proposals in the order of their probable efficacy to effect their purpose. I see no reason why the first—the coinage of sovereigns at Bombay—should have any effect at all towards increasing the use of sovereigns as currency. Four types of occasion can be distinguished on which gold bars might be presented at Bombay for coinage:—

(*a*) Gold might be deliberately imported from England for the purpose; or it might occasionally happen that importers of gold bars, having temporarily miscalculated the demand for bars, would wish to sell these bars to the Government.

(*b*) Owners of Indian gold mines might conceivably find it worth their while to suspend the arrangements they have made in recent years with English refiners and might sell their gold (about £2,000,000 annually) to the Bombay Mint. Whether or not they would find it worth while to do this would presumably depend on the facilities for refining in India and the terms offered by the Bombay Mint.

(*c*) The habits of the people might be changing, the importation of new bars from England ceasing, and the people wishing to get rid of the bars and ornaments they already had.

(*d*) In times of famine or depression the people might sell their bars and ornaments to the Mint when they were driven to turn their ultimate resources into money.

Provided the Bombay Mint did not offer to coin on more favourable terms than the British Mint, which presumably it would not do, it seems exceedingly unlikely that bar gold would be imported from England on purpose to be coined in India rather than in England. But if this were to happen, it would have no consequences worth thinking about. The place of mintage is a matter of indifference. In all the other eventualities, suggested above, the gold is brought to the Mint, not to satisfy a demand for new gold currency, but because the owners of the gold wish to sell it. The sellers would take payment in sovereigns, notes, or rupees (since the former can always be exchanged for the latter), as might suit their convenience. In cases (*c*) and (*d*) the Government would probably be forced in the end to export the sovereigns it had itself minted, and to bear the cost of export as well as the cost of minting.

The chief result of mintage at Bombay, therefore (assuming that the terms for coining were substantially the same as in England), would be a small saving of expense to sellers of gold in India. Importers of gold bars would be saved occasionally a small loss of interest due to miscalculation; owners of Indian gold mines might conceivably pay, at the expense of Government, infinitesimally higher dividends; the people turning their hoards into money would be able to save the expense of sending the gold to England. A corresponding cost would fall on the Government, for mintage in the first instance and sometimes for export afterwards. These consequences, whether desirable or not, have very little to do with currency questions. The last of them—the making it easier to turn hoards into money—is very likely desirable. But all of them could be brought about more cheaply without the establishment of a Bombay Mint. It would be sufficient if the Government were to publish terms on which it was ready to buy gold bars. It might be a real convenience if Government notified its readiness to purchase bars tendered in India at Rs. 58 annas 5 per ounce[1] (payable in silver or notes or sterling drafts on London or in sovereigns, on the present system, if they were available).[2] The Government would be involved, from time to time, in the cost of export; but this cost it would have to bear, I believe, just as often if there were a mint, while the cost of the mint itself would be saved. Such a notification, as is suggested above, would be much more in the true spirit of the Indian currency system than the establishment of a gold mint would be; and it would serve the convenience of the public just as efficiently, at less expense to Government. The establishment of a Mint, however, would flatter at small expense an ignorant vanity. The Government by granting it in response to popular appeal (though I doubt whether, in fact, there is any such appeal) would have a pleasant feeling of being democratic on an occasion when to yield involves no more evil than any other expenditure on a piece of fairly cheap ostentation.

13. To the second proposal for the mintage of a distinctively Indian gold coin many of the above comments apply equally. But the existence of a

[1] This corresponds to the Bank of England's normal price for gold bullion.

[2] At present notes can be issued by currency offices, but only to treasuries on the requisition of the Comptroller-General, in exchange for gold bullion at the rate of 1 rupee for 7·53344 grains troy of fine gold. Since April 1, 1907, the receipt at the Indian Mints of gold bullion and gold coins other than sovereigns and half-sovereigns has, in fact, been stopped by Government of India Notification.

10-rupee gold piece (13s. 4d.) might very possibly do something to popularise the use of gold as currency, largely because it would be of a smaller and therefore more convenient denomination.[1] It is very difficult to prophesy with regard to the local popularity of a new coin. On the other hand—apart from the general objections, to be dealt with later, against popularising gold—it is generally a bad thing to introduce a new coin and add to the confusion of currencies. For purposes of export, at times of depression, the 10-rupee piece would be worth less than two-thirds of a sovereign. The sovereign, moreover, is fast becoming the international gold coin *par excellence* far beyond the bounds of the British Empire. In 1911, 43,305,722 British sovereigns were minted, or a good deal more than the whole gold coinage in that year of the rest of the world, viz. £33,375,455. A rival coin ought not to be set up in India unless some evident advantage is to be obtained from it.

14. The third policy—that of active measures on the part of Government to get more gold into circulation—is not likely to be adopted. If it were, it is difficult to say if it would be successful or not. To force a coin on people is not always the best way to popularise it; and if rupees were to be refused, there would probably be a small premium on them

[1] I have, however, seen no evidence which suggests that *half*-sovereigns are specially popular on account of their lower denomination.

or a small discount on gold—a position which would not help gold.

15. It is probably the case, however, that if it were desirable to popularise the use of gold, a means could be found of effecting this in some degree. The main question is whether this is, in fact, the right policy. Lord Crewe looks forward (see his speech in the House of Lords, November 14, 1912) "with some confidence to the increased use of gold currency in India among the people, although it may be a long and indefinite time before it becomes the habitual and favourite coin in the country at large." Ought he to expect this result with satisfaction as well as confidence?

My own answer to this question is unhesitatingly in the negative. The principal arguments against such a policy are two,—first, the general argument that it is extravagant and wasteful to have gold coins as the actual media of circulation, and second, the argument, more especially applicable to India, that it would diminish, and not, as its advocates claim for it, increase the stability of the currency system as a whole.

16. Let us consider first how heavy a loss and expense the popularity of a gold currency might involve. During the last twelve years the Government have been able to accumulate a sum of about £21,000,000 sterling from the profits of rupee coinage; and the interest on the invested portion of the Paper Currency

Reserve is now about £300,000 annually. Thus the annual income, derivable from the interest on the sums set free by the use of cheap forms of currency, amounts already to about £1,000,000. With the rapidly increasing use of notes, this income should show a steady growth in the future. Both these sources of profit would be gravely jeopardised if the introduction of an Indian gold coin were to meet with any considerable measure of success. It would be specially unfortunate if a competitor to the paper currency were to be introduced, before the virtual abolition of the system of circles has had time to have its full effect in the direction of popularising the use of notes.

17. Advocates of a gold currency, however, would not, I think, deny that it might involve the country in some extra expense. They support their policy on the ground that it would do a great deal to ensure the stability of the currency system, and that it is worth while to incur some expense for this object. I think it is possible to show that such a policy is likely on the whole to have an exactly opposite effect.

It is suggested that the currency should be composed of rupees, gold, and paper, with rupees still predominating, but consisting of gold in a considerably higher proportion than at present. This greater infusion of gold would necessarily be at the expense either of the Currency Reserve or of the Gold Standard Reserve. If the gold replaced notes, the former would be diminished, and, if it replaced rupees, the latter.

It is tacitly assumed that the greater part of what has to be withdrawn from the circulation at a time of crisis would come from the gold portion of the circulation.

This assumption seems to me to be unwarranted and contrary to general experience. At a time of crisis it is the fiduciary coins with which the public are most eager to part. Bankers and others would keep as much of their surplus currency as they possibly could in the form of gold, and it would be rupees (in great part) and not gold that would be paid into the Government Treasuries.

Thus the infusion of more gold into the circulation would necessarily weaken the existing reserves and would not correspondingly reduce the amount of such reserves which Government ought in prudence to keep. When it became necessary to contract the volume of currency, Government would be in a *worse* position than at present, unless the greater part of what was withdrawn came from the gold portion of the circulation and not from the rupee or paper portion. This is not an expectation upon which it would be prudent to act.

I have already quoted the late Lord Goschen's authority in support of the centralisation of gold reserves. A further passage from the address he delivered on the same occasion (in proposing a scheme of one-pound notes for England) is relevant here:—"I would much prefer for national and monetary purposes to have £20,000,000 of gold under our command at the Bank of England than 30,000,000 sovereigns in the hands of the public. . . . If the issue (of one-pound notes) took place, and were taken up, we should have £20,000,000 more *central* gold—an immeasurably stronger reserve than 30,000,000 sovereigns on which we could not place our hands."

18. There are, in fact, two ways of maintaining stability in a country whose demand for currency varies widely from year to year—*either* it must consist almost *wholly* of gold, *or* a sufficient reserve must be *concentrated* in the hands of Government. If only one-quarter or one-fifth of the circulation consists of gold, I do not think that a Government can rely on getting more than a *fraction* of this, when it becomes necessary to contract the circulation by one-sixth or one-seventh; whereas if the gold is in the Government's reserves, the *whole* of it is available.

For obvious reasons of convenience and of economy the greater part of the Indian circulation must continue in any case to consist of rupees. It is vain to suppose that the advantages of a true gold currency can be obtained by the compromise of somewhat increasing the gold element. If the Government dissipates some part of its sterling resources over the country—and any proposal for a greater infusion of gold into the currency amounts to this—it must plainly stand in a weaker position to meet a crisis than if they are concentrated in its own chests.

19. The encouragement of gold, therefore, would involve expense, and, at the same time, diminish safety. There is a further argument against it, connected nevertheless with the above, which is of great importance.

If gold were to supplant rupees only and not notes, and were to supplant them to so great an extent that sovereigns would tend to flow out of the currency at times of depression, there might be something to be said for it. It is certainly the case that it is a disadvantageous thing for India to have so large a part of her currency in the form of expensive tokens,—the issue of rupees strengthens the reserves by less than a half of their nominal value. The degree of damage to the Government's reserves, therefore, would be much less if the gold were to supplant rupees than if it were to supplant notes. But this is most unlikely to be the case. It is for comparatively large payments that the sovereign may gradually come into use, and for these it is essentially a rival to the note. For small payments, which in India make in the aggregate an enormous total, the sovereign can no more supplant the rupee than it can supplant the shilling in England.

Reports collected by the Comptroller of Currency

in 1911–12 already show in a striking way the tendency of gold to take the place which is, or might be, occupied by notes. The rapidity with which gold is becoming popularised in the Punjab is probably due in very great part to the fact that notes have never become acclimatised there.[1] The inconvenience of making large payments in silver is obvious;[2] and facilities for obtaining gold are naturally welcomed. The events of the last two or three years may have done very great harm in the direction of postponing the development of the use of notes in Northern India. In Bengal and Eastern Bengal, on the other hand, the slow progress made by gold is to be explained by the fact that the people of these provinces are much more accustomed to the use of notes, which are even used in some cases for the purpose of hoarding (cf. p. 165). If the Government were to attempt to further in any way the circulation of gold in the Bengals, they would be aiming a dangerous blow at their own note issue; whereas if notes could be encouraged in place of rupees in the jute trade, there would be a huge increase in their circulation. It is also reported that the use of gold in the rice trade in Burma would displace notes

[1] The Manager of the National Bank in the Punjab reported in 1911–1912:—"The fact of currency notes having always been unpopular throughout the Punjab and, excepting in Lahore, being cashed only at a considerable discount, has no doubt conduced to the popularity of the sovereign. A portable medium commanding its full face value was urgently required and the sovereign has for the present met the want."

[2] £6000 in rupees weighs more than a ton.

mainly. The following quotations from the reports (collected in 1911–12 by the Comptroller of Currency from districts in the Punjab), referred to above, illustrate the point that gold is preferred to silver because it is more convenient to carry, and that notes are distrusted because there is no universally spread assurance of their ready convertibility.[1]

Gujranwala.—The zamindar prefers to have his price for the grain in gold, as he can easily carry it and easily exchange it and, if necessary, easily put it away. He shies at currency notes of any value, as they cannot be easily exchanged, and to receive payment in silver means cost of carriage and a greater risk of being robbed. Contractors of the Canal Department are very glad to receive payment of their cheques in gold. Some have remarked that sovereigns can be exchanged even in the village most remote from civilisation, but notes, even of the value of Rs. 5, are looked upon with distrust by the village yokel and even by the village sahukar. With a sovereign there is no trouble, no awkward questions are asked and no discount taken.

Jhang.—The people prefer gold because it is less troublesome than silver money.

Gurdaspur.—The facility of transit is the reason why corn merchants prefer sovereigns to silver.

Ambala.—Both in cities and villages, sovereigns are replacing notes more than rupees.

Bannu.—Gold is slowly but steadily replacing currency notes.

Rohtak.—(With the increase of gold) a corresponding decrease in the use of currency notes has been observed during 1911–12.

[1] The Government should probably instruct its officers to receive and change notes with freedom on every possible occasion, in order to dissipate this idea.

Ludhiana.—(With the increase of gold) the issues of notes have correspondingly decreased.

These particular statements are corroborated by general statistics. The most recent statistics of the use of 10-rupee notes in the Punjab and in Bombay, as compared with Bengal, strongly suggest that the recent development of gold circulation in these provinces has been at the expense of these notes. "In the Punjab it is reported (in 1911–12) that large payments for agricultural produce are never made in notes, and that gold is replacing notes to some extent even in ordinary payments among merchants and traders." In the light of these facts, it is a wonderful tribute to the enduring power of the "sound" currency maxims of the middle of last century that responsible officials should have welcomed the outflow of gold as the salvation of their system.

Before leaving this topic I wish to emphasise, in close connexion with it, a special reason why it is so important to develop the use of notes in India at the present time. It is desirable to encourage the popularity of the note issue, and to avoid encouraging its rivals, not only for reasons of immediate economy or because, by the centralisation of the reserves, the stability of the currency is increased, but also because, in a country where cheques are not likely for many years to come to be used to a dominating extent, it is only thus that a proper degree of seasonal elasticity in the currency can possibly be secured. This question has been already raised in Chapter III., and I shall return to it again in Chapters VI. and VII.

20. One minor indirect consequence of the existing system is worth reference. Gold flows into the Currency Reserve when this is a cheaper way of getting notes or rupees than by buying Council Bills or Transfers (see Chapter V.). It flows out of the Currency Reserve when sovereigns are wanted for circulation or for hoarding, or when this is the cheapest way in which bullion dealers can get gold. There is reason for thinking that a good deal flows out for the last reason, and it is the occasion of this outflow which I wish to examine in a little more detail. The Currency Department publishes figures which show the number of sovereigns withdrawn from the Treasuries each month. It appears from these that, while some are withdrawn in the winter months during the busy season, when the demand for currency and for hoarding (since it is then that the cultivators sell their crops and realise their savings in coin) is at its height, there is in the summer also, when it is most improbable that an extra supply is required for these purposes, a steady and, in the aggregate, a heavy drain. A brief arithmetical calculation provides what must, I think, be the explanation of this. Since the price of bullion in London is (normally) £3 : 17 : 9 per oz., while the price of

sovereigns is £3 : 17 : 10½, the bullion import point of Indian exchange will be a little below the sovereign import point. Thus when exchange is fairly high, an Indian purchaser of gold finds it more profitable to buy drafts on London, purchase gold in the bullion market and ship it to India, than to purchase sovereigns from the Treasury at 1s. 4d.; but when exchange is low, the reverse is the case and it is cheaper to get as much gold as the Treasury will let you have at 1s. 4d. I do not know exactly where the dividing line comes;[1] but when telegraphic transfers are at 1s. 4⅛d. it is certainly more profitable to get gold bullion in London, and when they are at 1s. 4$\frac{1}{32}$d. it may pay to get it in India.

These considerations are modified in practice by the fact that many Indian purchasers of bullion have a preference for small gold bars which are manufactured in England. Thus these bars are worth more than an equivalent weight of sovereigns, and consequently importation of bullion in this form takes place throughout the year. But for many non-currency purposes sovereigns are as good or nearly as good as other forms of bullion, and for these purposes the Indian Treasury is the bullion dealer's cheapest source of supply when exchange is relatively low. Thus in the summer months the bullion dealers will always draw their supplies from the Treasury, so long as the Treasury is willing to

[1] See pp. 113-118 for an account of the cost of transporting bullion to India.

supply them. Whenever, therefore, gold in India is available to the public throughout the year, the Government will lose during the summer months whatever amount the bullion dealers require. On every sovereign thus drawn out, the Government loses about 1½d. For the gold could have been kept in England by selling bills at a rate more advantageous than the par of exchange by about this amount. The annual amount which is drawn out by bullion dealers when gold is available all the year round is probably not less than £2,000,000. Thus an important indirect effect of the present practice is to allow bullion dealers in the summer months to get their gold at the Government's cost slightly cheaper than they otherwise could.

21. India, as we all know, already wastes far too high a proportion of her resources in the needless accumulation of the precious metals. The Government ought not to encourage in the slightest degree this ingrained fondness for handling hard gold. By the elimination of both precious metals, to the utmost extent that public opinion will permit, from amongst the hoards and the circulation of the country, they ought to counteract an uncivilised and wasteful habit.

It is interesting to reflect that India's love of the precious metals, ruinous though it has been to her own economic development, has flourished in the past to the great advantage of Western nations. Every one knows Jevons's description of India as the sink of the precious metals, always ready to absorb the redundant bullion of the West and to save Europe from the more violent disturbances to her price level. In very recent years, while the South African mines have been reaching the zenith of their production, she has been fulfilling to perfection her rôle of sink. Prices have been rising, as it is, much faster than is healthy and in a way very disadvantageous to such a creditor nation as Great Britain, to whom large sums fixed in terms of gold are annually due. It is reasonable to think that without the assistance of the Indian demand, they would have risen still faster. From its very short period point of view the City is sometimes cross when this Indian demand shows itself in an inconvenient week; but if we take a longer view the Indian demand is, at a time of plentiful gold supply like the present, a true friend to the City and an enemy of inflation.

On the other hand, if a time comes when Indians learn to leave off their unfertile habits and to divert their hoards into the channels of productive industry and to the enrichment of their fields, they will have the money markets of the world at their mercy. A surfeit of gold can do at least as much damage as a shortage. During the past sixty years India is supposed to have absorbed, in addition to her previous accumulations, more than £300,000,000 of gold (apart from enormous quantities of silver). We may presume that, if India ceases to demand fresh gold and begins to disgorge some part of her huge stock, she will do so gradually. Yet if the change comes at a time of big new production, she may involve the world, nevertheless, in a very great inflation of gold prices.

If, however, India is thus to turn the tables on the West, she must not delay too long. The time may not be far distant when Europe, having perfected her mechanism of exchange on the basis of a gold standard, will find it possible to regulate her standard of value on a more rational and stable basis. It is not likely that we shall leave permanently the most intimate adjustments of our economic organism at the mercy of a lucky prospector, a new chemical process, or a change of ideas in Asia.

CHAPTER V

COUNCIL BILLS AND REMITTANCE

1. REMITTANCE by means of what are termed Council Bills is a feature peculiar to the Indian system, and is not, so far as I know, to be paralleled elsewhere. It arises partly from the historical circumstance that the Government of India is the successor of a trading company, partly from the necessity under which the Government lies of making very large annual remittances to England.

2. The Home Charges, that is, the payments which the Government of India must make *in England*, for interest on debt, pensions, payments to the War Office, Government stores (not chargeable to capital), etc., amount to £19,000,000 or £20,000,000 annually. But the amount which it is necessary to remit, apart from extraordinary remittances to be dealt with later, is usually less than this; for the amount of new capital raised by Government in England usually exceeds their capital expenditure in this country on repayments and on railway materials, etc. Thus the amount which it is necessary to remit to England annually is from

£15,000,000 to £18,000,000. Rupees to this amount, being part of the revenue from taxation, etc., accumulate in the Indian Treasuries. This value is remitted to England by selling for sterling in London bills which can be cashed in rupees in Calcutta. Thus the Government of India pays out rupees in Calcutta when the bills are presented, and the Secretary of State's balances at the Bank of England are swelled by a corresponding amount.

The Government is, therefore, one of the largest dealers in foreign exchange, and does for itself business, which Colonial Governments, for example, who have a certain amount of similar transactions to carry through (though on a far smaller scale), would do through a bank. But while the Government saves for itself the commission which it would otherwise have to pay to a bank, it is not, in any real sense, a competitor with the banks for business. In the first place, it sells exchange, save in exceptional circumstances, in one direction only. And in the second place, the Secretary of State's method of selling exchange results in his dealing exclusively with the Exchange Banks and financial houses, and not directly with the trading public. The Secretary of State is in effect the ultimate source of supply for bills on India, and the banks, after securing what private bills are available, even up their demands for remittance to India by buying bills from him,—provided he is selling them at a rate which makes this form of remittance cheaper than the alternative one of sending sovereigns. The method by which these bills are sold is as follows.

3. The bills are offered in London for tender at the Bank of England every Wednesday morning, the Secretary of State for India in Council (or, for short, the India Council, whence the name Council Bills) having previously announced the amount (70 lakhs, say) for which tenders are invited. There is a reserve price (not published) below which he will not sell, but this reserve price is seldom operative.[1] The tenders name the amount tendered for and the number of pence per rupee which is offered. The total amount of 70 lakhs is then allotted to the highest bidders, the allotment at the minimum rate accepted being proportionate to the amount applied for at that rate.

If the demand is large and the minimum rate of allotment high (say 1s. $4\frac{3}{32}$d.), the amount offered for tender the following week (which is announced at the same time as the result of the previous allotment) is likely to be increased. In the interval between the allotments on successive Wednesdays, the Secretary of State is usually willing to sell what are known as "specials" at a rate $\frac{1}{32}$d. higher than the highest rate of allotment on the preceding Wednesday.

4. It should be added that cash must be paid for

[1] It was operative, however, in the middle of March 1913, when the whole amount offered was not allotted, tenders below 1s. 4d. being rejected; later in the month tenders below 1s. 4d. were accepted.

the bills in London as soon as they are allotted; but, on account of the time taken by the mail, they cannot be changed into rupees at Calcutta for about a fortnight. A fortnight's interest is therefore lost, and it is worth paying extra to obtain what are called "telegraphic transfers," by means of which rupees can be obtained at Calcutta almost as soon as the sovereigns are paid into the Secretary of State's account at the Bank of England.

The Secretary of State, therefore, is usually willing to sell telegraphic transfers at a rate $\frac{1}{32}$d. per rupee higher than the rate for bills.[1] If the purchaser chooses transfers, the effect to him is that he gets his rupees a fortnight earlier in India and pays for this privilege a sum equal to 5 per cent on the money for a fortnight. The question, whether it is worth the purchaser's while to pay this extra sum, chiefly depends upon the Indian bank rate, because this governs the amount of interest which can be gained by having the money immediately available in India. It may happen, of course, that a particular bank may have a special urgency for funds in India, or that the rate for fortnightly loans does not closely agree with the bank rate. Generally speaking, however, if the purchaser can lend money out at no higher rate than

[1] The rule is supposed to be that the extra charge for transfers is $\frac{1}{32}$d. per rupee when the Indian bank rate is below 9 per cent, and $\frac{1}{16}$d. when it is 9 per cent or above. The last occasions, on which the difference of $\frac{1}{16}$d. was in force, occurred between December 1906 and March 1907. In 1904 and formerly the $\frac{1}{16}$d. difference came into force when the Indian bank rate exceeded 6 per cent.

3 per cent in India, he will certainly prefer bills; but if he can lend at 7 per cent in India, it will be more profitable for him to buy transfers.

Experience accords with these expectations. When the Indian bank rate is high and the difference of $\frac{1}{32}$d. between the two prices is in force, the demand is almost entirely for transfers. This is convenient to bankers, and, if he has the rupees waiting in India, profitable to the Secretary of State.

5. The bills and transfers are made payable at the option of the purchaser at Calcutta, Bombay, or Madras. The amount drawn on Madras is relatively small, and Calcutta comes first, with about 45 per cent of the whole.

6. Up to 1900 the volume of sales of Council Bills in any year was mainly governed by the amount required to defray the Home Charges, this amount partly depending on the volume of capital borrowings in the year. But the sales also fluctuated, though within comparatively narrow limits in most years, according to the Secretary of State's opportunities (depending on the activity of business and the balance of trade) of selling his bills at a satisfactory rate. Since 1900, however, the functions of the Council Bill system have been enlarged, and it has now become a very important part of the general mechanism for the maintenance of the Gold Exchange Standard.

7. The way in which this has arisen is easily

explained. On account of the provision by which rupees can always be obtained in India in exchange for sovereigns at the rate of 1s. 4d. per rupee, it can never be worth while for the banks to buy Council Bills at a price which exceeds 1s. 4d. by more than the cost of sending gold to India. This cost varies considerably from time to time, but it seldom exceeds $\frac{1}{8}$d. If, therefore, the Secretary of State refuses to sell bills at less than 1s. 4$\frac{1}{8}$d., when the banks are requiring to remit to India, gold will flow. This gold will be presented at the Treasuries in India to be exchanged for rupees or notes. Thus the only effect of the Secretary of State's refusing to sell remittances at a price which suits the banks is that sterling resources accumulate in his Treasuries in India instead of in England. This may not be convenient to him. For example, if the banks are sending gold to India on a large scale and are exchanging it for rupees, a time may come when this demand can only be met by minting more rupees; the silver for this must be purchased in London and the profit on the coinage must be credited to the Gold Standard Reserve which, for reasons to be discussed in the next chapter, is kept for the most part in London; thus the gold has eventually to be shipped back again to England to pay for the silver and to be credited to the Gold Standard Reserve. In this case a double loss is involved—the cost of sending the gold to India (for the Secretary of State could probably have got

1s. 4⅛d. per rupee if he had sold transfers, whereas if gold flows he gets only 1s. 4d.) and the cost of bringing it back again, say, $\frac{3}{32}$d.; thus a refusal to sell bills would mean an eventual loss of nearly ¼d. per rupee or about 1½ per cent. Or, again, the policy of holding some part of the gold in the Currency Reserve in London for possible use in emergency, may lead to the Secretary of State's preferring gold to accumulate in London rather than in India; otherwise it will have to be sent back again, in pursuance of this policy, and a double loss incurred, as in the former case. Lastly, if the Secretary of State has considerable cash balances in India, it may be worth his while for a time to cash additional Council Bills out of these, thus in effect transferring his balances to London. The reasons that may make him inclined to do this are, first, that to increase the proportion of his cash balances held in sterling puts him in a stronger position in a case of emergency; second, that selling Council Bills at a good price now will enable him to meet the Home Charges later on when he might not be able to sell his Bills at so good a price (in this case the transference of cash balances from India to London is only temporary); third, that it may put him in a stronger position for carrying out impending loan transactions at the most favourable moment; and fourth, that cash balances held in London can be made to earn a small rate of interest.

All these considerations being taken into account,

it can only be worth the Secretary of State's while to refuse to sell bills within the gold export price, when he deliberately wishes either to increase his cash balances in India at the expense of his balances in London, or to replenish that part of the gold portion of the Currency Reserve which is kept in India

Thus he will endeavour to make as certain as possible of selling within the year the amount budgeted for (*i.e.*, the Home Charges adjusted with reference to the probable capital transactions of the year and the state of the cash balances); but he will sell more than this if the demand for remittance is so great that, on his refusal to sell, the price of remittance will rise to the gold export point. In the words of the annual budget, "the *estimate* of Council drawings is for the amount necessary to provide for the Secretary of State's requirements, but additional bills will be sold if needed to meet the demands of trade."

8. Let us sum up the argument so far, and enforce at the same time the contention, brought up at the end of Chapter I., that the volume of currency circulating in India does not depend, as some critics have maintained, on the caprice of the India Office in the amount of Council Bills that it offers for sale. So far as Council Bills are sold for the ordinary purposes of remittance of Government funds from India to London, they are cashed in India out of the general balances of Government. But when they

are sold in larger quantities, to obviate the necessity of sovereigns being sent, sufficient rupees are not forthcoming from this source. One expedient is to pay out some of the rupees in the Paper Currency Reserve or in the silver branch of the Gold Standard Reserve, and to pay an equivalent sum into the branches of these reserves which are held in London, "earmarked" at the Bank of England,[1] or in other sterling forms. If, on the other hand, the India Council had refused to sell bills freely, gold would have been exported to India, taken to the Paper Currency Department, and exchanged for rupees in notes or silver. In either case there is a similar increase in the volume of currency in India not held by the Government. The volume of currency which finds its way into circulation in India is, therefore, quite independent of the Secretary of State's action. Exceptional amounts of Council Bills are only sold when exchange has reached a point at which it is nearly as profitable to remit gold; and if Council Bills were not sold sovereigns would go instead (the expense of sending them being lost), for which the Government of India would have to give rupees in exchange. This point is important, for it is often assumed in controversy regarding

[1] Thus a probable effect of exceptionally large sales of Council Bills is an earmarking of gold on Indian account at the Bank of England. The extent to which the Indian system can be misunderstood is well illustrated by the fact that in a money article recently published in an important newspaper in this country, an increased offering of bills by the India Council was given as a reason for expecting a *postponement* of the need for earmarking gold at the Bank on Indian account.

the currency and its relation to prices that the issue of rupees into circulation depends in some way upon the amount of Council Bills sold by the Government, and can, therefore, be expanded or contracted by them at will, according to the policy of the moment. Broadly speaking, this is false. Even if the Government were to hasten the flow of rupees into circulation by selling an exceptional quantity of bills at a relatively low rate (which would be equivalent to lowering by a fraction of a penny the normal value of the rupee as measured in sterling), and were to pursue this policy over a long period, the permanent effect could be no more than in proportion to the amount by which they had thus lowered the par value of the rupee in terms of sterling. This is the amount of their conceivable executive power, if the Government were to exercise it. In fact, it has not been exercised.

If, however, the stock of rupees in the reserves is running low (for a considerable quantity of rupees must always be kept there in order to ensure the ready convertibility of the notes in terms of rupees), and more Council Bills are sold in London than can be conveniently cashed in Calcutta in the above ways, more rupees must be issued from the Mint. The silver out of which they are minted is purchased in England out of the proceeds of selling the additional Council Bills, and the surplus due to the fact that rupees are worth more than the silver they contain, is credited to the Gold Standard Reserve.

According to the present practice the process in these circumstances also is, therefore, automatic, and the amount of new rupees put into circulation does not depend on the arbitrary action of the Secretary of State in selling or withholding Council Bills. If he did not sell bills, sovereigns would be sent to India, new rupees would have to be coined to meet the obligation under which the Government of India has placed itself of giving rupees in exchange for sovereigns on demand, and a great part of the sovereigns would have to be credited in some form or other to the Gold Standard Reserve or shipped back to England again to pay for the silver.

It is true that, if a different practice were adopted (a practice which was adopted in part in 1907), and if the profits on the coinage of rupees, instead of being credited to the Gold Standard Reserve, were turned into rupees and spent by the Government in India on goods and services (whether for capital or any other purpose), more rupees would be in circulation for the time being than would have been the case otherwise. But even in this case the effect on the volume of circulation must be temporary, so long as the provisions for the maintenance of the rupee at 1s. 4d. are in operation. For this additional issue of rupees would, eventually, have the effect of delaying additional demands for coinage in the future or of precipitating an occasion for the withdrawal of rupees from circulation.

While, therefore, it is to a certain extent within the power of Government (though not at present according to their usual practice) to urge a certain number of rupees into circulation *more rapidly* than is necessary, they cannot *permanently* increase the circulation without depreciating its gold value, that is, they cannot permanently increase the circulation beyond what it would otherwise be and at the same time maintain the rupee at 1s. 4d. It may be added that a release of rupees from any other reserve, or even a temporary increase in the amount of capital funds annually raised by Government abroad for use in India, would have a similar effect to the release of rupees from the Gold Standard Reserve. But, however all this might be, at present the Government of India do *not*, in fact, exert such discretionary powers as they possess for affecting, even temporarily, the volume of circulation.

9. I have said that the cost of sending gold to India does not generally exceed $\frac{1}{8}$d. per rupee. The Secretary of State has, therefore, a standing notification (since January 1904) that he will sell bills at 1s. 4$\frac{1}{8}$d. Up to January 1900 he undertook to sell telegraphic transfers at 1s. 4$\frac{5}{32}$d. without limit of quantity, and since that time he has usually been willing to do so.[1] The cost of sending gold to India

[1] On two occasions this practice has been suspended—in January 1900, when the price rose to 1s. 4$\frac{3}{8}$d., and in December 1906–March 1907, when it rose to 1s. 4$\frac{3}{16}$d. The reason for the suspension in the second case was the operation of the rule by which the premium charged for telegraphic

depends, however, on complex causes, varying considerably from time to time, and is often a good deal less than ⅛d. It is not easy, therefore, for the Secretary of State to know at exactly what price gold will become a serious competitor of bills as a means of remittance; and not infrequently Council Bills are, unintentionally, at a price which makes it cheaper to send gold. It will be interesting to consider briefly the kinds of causes which influence the gold import point.[1]

10. The expense of remitting gold from one country to another is made up of insurance, freight, and loss of interest. Even the first item is sometimes capable of variation. For example, after the recent robbery of sovereigns in transit from London to Alexandria, the ordinary rate quoted on gold, consigned by the route (Bremen and Trieste) by which the stolen gold had been sent, was doubled, rising from 1s. 3d. to 2s. 6d. per cent. Again, on one recent occasion, it was stated that more gold would have been shipped if it had not been for the fact that the mail-boat was already carrying a million and a half sterling in gold and silver, the underwriters requiring a higher premium than usual if

---

transfers over the rate for bills depends on the Indian bank rate (see p. 105). The statement made in answer to a question on this subject in the House of Commons (April 30, 1912) by the Parliamentary Under-Secretary was not quite correct.

[1] Old-fashioned treatises on the foreign exchanges often leave the student with the impression that the gold import point is a known and stable thing given for good in books of reference. How far this is from the truth, the example of India well illustrates.

they were to insure a larger sum than this on a single voyage. But if it is a matter of shipping sovereigns *from England* the variations in the cost of insurance and freight are relatively small. The *main* part of variation in the gold point arises either out of the possibility of getting sovereigns *from other sources*, or from variations in the rate of interest.

These other sources are either sovereigns in transit from Australia or sovereigns ready for export from Egypt. As India lies between Australia and England, it is naturally cheaper (mainly on account of the smaller loss of interest) to send sovereigns from Australia to India than from Australia to England. Let us suppose that the state of the Australian exchanges is such that it pays to remit sovereigns from Australia to London anyhow, and assume, for the sake of simplicity (and without, in fact, any substantial sacrifice of truth), that the cost of freight and insurance from Australia to London is the same as from Australia to India. Now if, when the Australian sovereigns are off India, the bank which is remitting them can receive cash in London against their delivery in India, it will get its money at least a fortnight sooner, and will probably accept, therefore, about 1s. $3\frac{31}{32}$d. in London for 1s. 4d. delivered in India ($\frac{1}{32}$d. being the interest on 1s. 4d. for a fortnight at 5 per cent per annum). Gold bought in this way for immediate delivery in India is as good as a telegraphic transfer, *i.e.*, is worth $\frac{1}{32}$d. per rupee more than Council Bills. If, therefore, Council Bills are at a price in excess of 1s. $3\frac{1}{16}$d., gold about to be shipped from Australia competes with them as a means of remittance to India. Normally, of course, an Australian bank is able to get more than 1s. $3\frac{1}{16}$d. for gold delivered in India. I mean only that the Secretary of State cannot hope to undercut Australian gold, when it is available for export in large quantities, unless he is prepared to put down his price for Council Bills to this level. If, in these circumstances, he wants the gold in England rather than in India, his cheapest course, therefore, is to buy the gold in transit himself for delivery in England, by selling for it telegraphic transfers at a suitable rate.[1] This was done on a large scale in 1905–6 and 1906–7.

Surplus gold from Egypt is not capable of undercutting Council Bills so seriously as surplus gold from Australia; for in this case it is Egypt which lies in between. If we assume, for the sake of precise illustration,[2] that the cost of sending gold from Egypt to London is nearly the same as that of sending it from Egypt to India, an Egyptian bank, about to ship sovereigns in any case, will take any price in excess of 1s. 4d.[3] paid in London for the delivery

[1] It is worth his while to do this, because the cost of sending gold from Australia to London in one transaction is less than the cost of sending it first from Australia to India and then from India to London in two separate transactions.

[2] I make this assumption, which is not exactly accurate, for purposes of illustration only.

[3] Or less, if paid at the time of shipment and in advance of the time of delivery.

in India of the value in gold of a rupee. This is the extreme case. If Council Bills are at a higher rate than 1s. 4d., say at 1s. $4\frac{1}{16}$d., the Alexandrian exchanges may be at a level which makes it profitable to ship gold from Egypt to India for payment in London, when it is not profitable to ship gold from Egypt to London. If we still make the above illustrative (but not exactly accurate) assumption, when Council Bills are at about 1s. $4\frac{1}{16}$d. and the Alexandrian exchange on London below par, Egyptian gold competes with Councils as a means of remittance to India. Of course the supply of remittance from this source is usually somewhat limited; when some Egyptian gold has flowed away to India under the influence of the above conditions, this is likely to have the effect of strengthening the Alexandrian exchange, and therefore, by modifying the conditions, of making the continuance of a flow less likely. The Egyptian gold is of great practical importance, because the busy season in Egypt comes rather earlier than the busy season in India, so that in the winter months the gold which has served the purpose of moving the crops in Egypt can be sent on to be changed into rupees which are to serve the same purpose in India. Of the gold, therefore, which flows from London to Egypt every autumn, very little finds its way back again to London; what is not kept by the cultivators in Egypt travels on in due course to India. The precise moment at which this movement takes place and its extent depend, as we have seen above, on the rate at which Council Bills are being sold in London, and also upon whether the Egyptian cotton crop is dealt with late or early. But when towards the end of their busy season the Egyptian banks find themselves with more gold than they need, Council Bills must be sold at a relatively low rate if the flow of this gold to India is to be prevented. The dealings between the Egyptian and the Indian banks must thus present very delicate problems of arbitrage.

It is probably within the power of the Secretary of State, if he wishes, to regulate the flow of gold direct from London to Bombay by means of the sales of Council Bills. But when gold is available in Australia or Egypt, the matter is not susceptible of such easy control.

The remaining element which determines the cost of remittance—variation in the market rate of interest—has been dealt with already. $\frac{1}{32}$d. represents the interest on 1s. 4d. for a fortnight at 5 per cent per annum. It is easy to calculate how the gold export point is affected by fluctuations in the market rate of discount in India on either side of 5 per cent.

11. So far we have been dealing with the upper limit of exchange and with the results of a heavy demand for Council Bills. The effects at the lower limit differ in this important respect, that the Government are under no legal obligation to prevent the deprecia-

tion of the rupee, and have not undertaken to give sovereigns for rupees in the way that they have undertaken to give rupees for sovereigns. There is nothing in law, therefore, to prevent exchange from falling indefinitely. There has been no change in law in this respect since 1895, when exchange actually did fall below 1s. 1d. The Government has, however, practically pledged its word to do all in its power to prevent the depreciation of the gold value of the rupee and to prevent exchange from falling below the lower limit of 1s. $3\frac{29}{32}$d. The business community would rightly regard it as a breach of faith if the Government were to permit exchange to fall below this rate, unless all reasonable resources had been exhausted.

12. We now see how intimately the management of Council Bills and of Government remittance is bound up with the Gold-Exchange Standard. The disadvantages from the point of view of regulating a Gold-Exchange Standard, which arise out of there being no Government bank, are partly compensated by the Secretary of State's being the largest dealer in foreign exchange. By regulating the amount of bills he offers for tender, he is able to regulate to a great extent the level of exchange. When exchange is falling below par he can support it by greatly restricting his offers; and if he cannot get at least 1s. $3\frac{29}{32}$d. for his bills, he withdraws from the market. In the meantime, of course, he has payments to make in England, while on the other hand rupees accumulate

in India, as the revenue flows in and no Council Bills are presented for payment. If the cash balances in London are not sufficient to stand the drain on them, gold at the Bank of England may be "un-earmarked" and placed to the Secretary of State's current account, rupees in India being transferred at the same time from the Government balances to the silver portion of the Paper Currency Reserve—the reverse process from that which has been described already as the result of exceptionally large sales of Council Bills.

If the Secretary of State's withdrawal from the market and the consequent scarcity of bills on India is insufficient to support exchange at 1s. $3\frac{29}{32}$d., more drastic measures are necessary. The method adopted on the last occasion of this kind was the offer by the Government of India in Calcutta of *sterling bills on London* at the rate of 1s. $3\frac{29}{32}$d., these bills being cashed in London out of the Gold Standard Reserve.

These measures were sufficient during the severe crisis of 1908. Their sufficiency for the future will be discussed in Chapter VI. in dealing with the Secretary of State's Reserves.

13. If we turn from the mechanism of remittance to the question of Government remittance as a whole, this can be explained most clearly by reference to a hypothetical India Office balance-sheet. The whole account for the year balances out in some such manner as this :—

PAYMENTS

Home Charges	x
Gold "earmarked," or securities bought for Currency Reserve in London	y
Cost of silver + profit on coinage credited to Gold Standard Reserve in London	z
Expenditure on stores in London for capital purposes in India	v
Transfer of cash balances from India to London . . .	$\pm w$
	$x+y+z+v\pm w$

RECEIPTS

Council Bills cashed from balances in India	$x-u+v\pm w$
Council Bills cashed from rupees in Currency Reserve in India	y
Council Bills cashed from new coinage	z
Total Council Bills drawn	$x+y+z-u+v\pm w$
Net capital borrowings in London	u
Total receipts in London	$x+y+z+v\pm w$

14. I will conclude this chapter with some statistics.

	1909-10.	1910-11.	1911-12.	1912-13 (revised estimate
	£	£	£	£
Home Charges (net)[1] .	18,763,000	18,003,000	18,333,000	18,986,000
Capital expenditure in England on material for railways and irrigation works	5,748,000	5,188,000	5,083,000	7,077,000
Credited to Gold Standard Reserve in England[2] .	8,090,000	600,000	...	1,200,000
Credited to Paper Currency Reserve in England .	1,000,000	2,545,000	1,988,000	400,000
Purchase of silver . .	...	...	...	7,059,000
Addition to Cash Balances in England[3] . . .	4,815,000	3,898,000	1,693,000	...
	38,416,000	30,234,000	27,097,000	34,722,000
Council Bills and Transfers	27,096,000[4]	26,783,000	27,058,000	25,760,000
Gold from India . .	...	...	...	1,928,000
Net debt incurred in England[5]	11,320,000	3,451,000	39,000	−2,983,000
Reduction of Cash Balances in England . . .	...	...	...	10,017,000
	38,416,000	30,234,000	27,097,000	34,722,000

[1] After deduction of certain small sources of revenue in England and various minor adjustments. [2] Apart from dividends earned and reinvested in England.

[3] Excluding balances in Gold Standard Reserve.

[4] Deducting bills on London sold in India.

[5] Excluding reduction of debt by annuities and sinking funds included in Home Charges.

The table given above analyses the Home Accounts in a way which brings out the essential facts more clearly than the Government's own published accounts. These actual figures may be compared with the hypothetical balance-sheet given in § 13.

The principal items of the Home Charges are analysed below. As these do not vary much from year to year it has been thought sufficient to give the figures of one recent year, namely, 1911–12. It will be seen that in that year about £5,000,000 was spent on pensions and leave allowances, £11,000,000 on debt services, and £2,250,000 on military services (excluding pensions). Other expenses were of a very small amount.

ANALYSIS OF HOME CHARGES IN 1911–12

Superannuation and pensions (Civil)		£2,063,100
,, ,, (Military) (net)		2,471,400
Furlough allowances		426,500
Interest on ordinary debt		2,284,700
Interest on railway debt and on capital deposited by companies		5,268,600
Railway annuities and sinking funds		3,623,600
Military services (apart from pensions)		2,277,400
Miscellaneous		1,130,200
		£19,545,500
Revenue from interest	£448,000	
Miscellaneous revenue	141,600	
		589,600
		£18,955,900

The total drawings of Council Bills, the average, maximum and minimum rates of allotment, and the fluctuation between the maximum and minimum in recent years were as follows :—

	Total Drawings of Council Bills.	Average Rate.	Maximum Rate.	Minimum Rate.	Fluctuation.
	£	d.	d.	d.	d.
1901–02	18,500,000	15·987	16·125	15·875	·250
1902–03	18,500,000	16·002	16·156	15·875	·281
1903–04	23,900,000	16·049	16·156	15·875	·281
1904–05	24,400,000	16·045	16·156	15·970	·186
1905–06	31,600,000	16·042	16·156	15·937	·219
1906–07	33,400,000	16·084	16·1875	15·937	·250
1907–08	15,300,000	16·029	16·1875	15·875	·312
1908–09	13,900,000	15·964	16	15·875	·125
1909–10	27,400,000	16·041	16·156	15·875	·281
1910–11	26,500,000	16·061	16·156	15·875	·281
1911–12	27,100,000	16·082	16·156	15·937	·219
1912–13	25,700,000	16·058	16·156	15·970	·186

CHAPTER VI

THE SECRETARY OF STATE'S RESERVES AND THE CASH BALANCES

1. The Indian authorities have undertaken a double responsibility. They must be prepared to supply rupees in payment for Council Bills or in exchange for sovereigns. And on the other hand they must be prepared also to supply sterling or sterling drafts in exchange for rupees. The maintenance of the Indian system depends on their ability to fulfil this double obligation to whatever extent may be required of them.

The objects to be attained are simple, but the methods of the Government are, largely for historical reasons, exceedingly complicated. I will discuss, first, the nature of the existing methods; second, their adequacy for their purpose; third, some proposals for making them more orderly and intelligible; and lastly, the management of the cash balances.

2. From the profits of rupee coinage[1] a reserve has been built up expressly for the purpose of sup-

[1] See p. 37 (footnote).

porting exchange. This is known as the Gold Standard Reserve. As the reserve is used in practice, not only for holding sterling reserves but also for holding a part of the rupee reserve, this title is a misnomer.[1]

For some years after the closing of the Mints no fresh coinage was undertaken. By 1900 it had become necessary to mint additional rupees, and from that time until 1907 the profits on coinage rapidly raised the Gold Standard Reserve to a respectable total. The crisis of 1907–8 made it necessary to withdraw a great number of rupees from circulation, and no further coinage was necessary on a significant scale until the autumn of 1912. By October 1912 the aggregate profits arising from coinage amounted to about £18,600,000. Of this, however, about £1,100,000 was diverted in 1907 for capital expenditure on railways—leaving about £17,500,000 for the Gold Standard Reserve. In addition to this the receipts on account of interest on that part which was invested amounted to about £3,250,000, against which is to be set about £1,000,000 depreciation in the value of the investments in October 1912 as compared with their original cost. Thus at that date this reserve stood at about £19,750,000, allowing for depreciation. During the winter of 1912–13 profits on the heavy issues of coinage caused a further increase, and we

[1] The designation of the reserve was changed from "Gold Reserve" to "Gold Standard Reserve" in 1906, when it was decided to hold a part in silver; but the change of title has not really made the position much clearer.

may conveniently think of the Gold Standard Reserve as being worth about £21,000,000 net at the end of 1912.

Of this total the greater part was held in sterling securities — about £16,000,000 (market price). In recent times the policy has been followed of holding at least half of this in securities of the most liquid possible type. On March 31, 1912, £4,500,000 was held in British Treasury Bills, and £4,735,600 in Exchequer Bonds. Of the rest about £7,000,000 (face value) was in Consols and other stock guaranteed by the British Government, and about £1,500,000 (face value) in various Colonial Government Securities.

Apart from the £16,000,000 thus invested, about £1,000,000 was, at the end of 1912, lent at short notice in the London Money Market; about £3,750,000 was held in India in rupees; and £250,000 in gold was "earmarked" at the Bank of England. The holding of some part in actual gold in England was an innovation introduced in November 1912.

It has been announced that the Gold Standard Reserve is to be allowed to accumulate through coinage profits and interest receipts until it stands at £25,000,000, and that £5,000,000 of this will be held in gold.[1] It is possible that when this figure has been reached, some part of its income may be applied to capital expenditure on railways. This would be a

[1] At the end of March 1913, £1,620,000 in gold stood to the credit of the Gold Standard Reserve in London.

reversion to the policy of 1907–8, since abandoned, when one-half of the profits of coinage was thus diverted.

The form in which the Gold Standard Reserve is held has been subject to much criticism. But it will not be useful to consider this until we are in a position to deal with the reserves as a whole.

3. The second reserve is the Paper Currency Reserve held against the note issue. The constitution of this has been explained in Chapter III. The invested portion may not exceed a stated maximum, of which a part only may be held in sterling securities and the rest must be placed in rupee securities. The whole of the balance must be held in gold or silver bullion, rupees, or sovereigns. But the gold may be held either in London or in India. The actual form in which the Currency Reserve was held at the end of December 1912 was approximately as follows:—

Sterling securities	£2,500,000
Rupee securities	6,500,000
Gold in London	7,250,000
Gold in India	17,500,000
Rupees in India	8,500,000
Silver bullion in India or in transit	1,500,000
	£43,750,000

4. The Government's remaining reserve source of supply of cash in the form of rupees or sterling is the Cash Balances. Both the total of these and the proportions held in rupees and sterling respectively vary within wide limits from time to time. Their total

amount fluctuates according to the volume of taxes coming in at different seasons of the year, the recency with which loans have been contracted for capital expenditure, the proximity of extraordinary expenditure impending, the receipts of windfalls of income (as, recently, from the opium revenue), the general prosperity of the country, and the degree of caution or optimism which, in the opinion of those responsible for the finances, the general situation warrants. The proportions held in rupees and sterling respectively depend even more on considerations of temporary convenience,—recent or impending capital transactions in London, the likelihood of sterling funds being wanted for the purchase of silver, and trade demands for Council Bills as a means of remittance. The totals of the cash balances at various dates are given below.

CASH BALANCES [1]

	In India.	In London.	Total.
March 31, 1901	£8,767,687	£4,091,926	£12,859,613
" 1903	12,081,388	5,767,786	17,849,174
" 1905	10,597,770	10,262,581	20,860,351
" 1907	10,026,932	5,606,812	15,633,744
" 1908	12,851,413	4,607,266	17,458,679
" 1909	10,235,483	7,983,898	18,219,381
" 1910	12,295,428	12,799,094	25,094,522
" 1911	13,566,922	16,696,990	30,263,912
" 1912	12,279,689	18,390,013	30,669,702
" 1913	19,543,900	8,372,900	27,916,800

[1] Excluding balances held in the Gold Standard Reserve.

It may be added that the Indian cash balances

are kept partly in District Treasuries all over the country, partly in Reserve Treasuries, and partly on deposit at the Presidency Banks. The District Treasuries do not usually contain more resources than they require for ordinary transactions, and the balances in excess of immediate requirements, which are transferred to the Reserve Treasuries, are mainly held in the form of notes. Thus the Government has no large surplus stock of rupees outside the Currency Reserve. The London Balances are held partly at the Bank of England and partly on loan for short periods with certain financial houses on an approved list.[1] No more than a working balance (about £500,000) is ordinarily held at the Bank of England, and this has been reckoned for many years now (though not formerly) amongst the "other" deposits, not amongst the "public" deposits. It will be seen from the table given above that the London Balances fell to a low level in 1908, the Secretary of State making free use of them to aid him in supporting exchange during the critical months of that year. On October 30, 1908, these balances had sunk to £1,196,691. In 1911 and 1912, on the other hand, they reached a very high figure, and in June of both these years exceeded £19,000,000. By the end of 1912 they had sunk again to a more normal level. This abnormally high level in the first half of 1912 gave rise to much criticism in regard

[1] See also pp. 190, 191, below.

both to the amount of the balances and also to the method adopted of lending them out in the London Money Market. Something will be said about this in the concluding paragraphs of this chapter.

5. We are now in a position to see exactly what resources in sterling and rupees respectively the Indian authorities have, on which to draw for the fulfilment of their currency obligations. Since the surplus balances in India, beyond those required by the District Treasuries and those deposited with the Presidency Banks, are mainly held in notes, we may neglect them for the present purpose.

Rupee Reserves are held partly in the Currency Reserve, partly in the Gold Standard Reserve. In December 1912 the amounts were approximately as follows:—

Currency Reserve[1]	£10,000,000
Gold Standard Reserve . . .	3,750,000
	£13,750,000

Sterling Reserves are held partly in the Currency Reserve, partly in the Gold Standard Reserve, and partly in the London Cash Balances. The forms in which they are held are gold (in the Currency Reserve, both in India and London, and to a small extent in the Gold Standard Reserve), money lent at short notice (in the Gold Standard Reserve and in the Cash Balances), and sterling securities (in the Currency

[1] Including silver bullion in India or in transit.

Reserve and in the Gold Standard Reserve). In December 1912 the amounts were approximately as follows :—

Gold—	
Currency Reserve in India . .	£17,500,000
Currency Reserve in London . .	7,250,000
Gold Standard Reserve in London .	250,000
	£25,000,000
Money at Short Notice—	
Gold Standard Reserve in London .	£1,000,000
Cash Balances in London . .	7,500,000
	£8,500,000
Sterling Securities—	
Currency Reserve	£2,500,000
Gold Standard Reserve . . .	16,000,000
	£18,500,000
Aggregate Sterling Resources—	
Gold	£25,000,000
Money at Short Notice . . .	8,500,000
Securities	18,500,000
	£52,000,000

6. Before we consider the adequacy of these reserves for their purposes, it will be useful to recall the circumstances of the two recent occasions on which their resources were severely taxed. The Government were hard pressed to supply sufficient rupees in 1906, and hard pressed to supply sufficient sterling in 1908. We can deal with both these occasions in a continuous narrative.

The coinage of rupees recommenced on a significant scale in 1900. For the five years following there was a steady annual demand for fresh coinage (low in 1901–2, high in 1903–4, but at no time abnormal) and the Mints were able to meet it with time to spare, though there was some slight difficulty in 1903–4. In 1905–6 the demand quickened, and from July 1905, when the Government's silver reserves stood at what was then considered the comfortable figure of 1837 lakhs[1] (£12,250,000), it quite outstript the new supplies arising from the mintage of the uncoined silver reserve. The Government were very slow to buy more silver and, in fact, do not seem to have taken steps to do so until, in December 1905, their bullion reserve was quite exhausted. They had then to buy silver in London hurriedly and at rather a high price. In the meantime the rupee reserves had sunk to the very low figure of 761 lakhs (*i.e.*, about 40% of the holdings six months earlier), and the demand for Council Bills in London, which would have to be cashed in rupees in India, showed no signs of abating. In order to give themselves breathing space, and to allow time for the silver recently bought in London to reach India and be coined, the Government had to raise the price of telegraphic transfers to what was then the unusually high figure of $1/4\frac{5}{32}$. This was the worst that happened. The new coinage very quickly overtook and passed the demand, and by the end of March 1906 the available silver reserves were double what they had been in January.

[1] Reckoning uncoined silver at its coined value.

This slight scare, however, was more than sufficient to make the Government lose their heads. Having once started on a career of furious coinage, they continued to do so with little regard to considerations of ordinary prudence—though their sins did not overtake them immediately. Without waiting to see how the busy season of 1906–7 would turn out, they coined heavily throughout the summer months, and, there being more silver in hand than could be conveniently held in the Currency Reserve, it was maintained, at the expense of the sterling resources, in the Gold Standard Reserve. In July 1906 the silver reserve stood at about 3200 lakhs. As a matter of fact the season of 1906–7 turned out well, and the demand for rupees was on a large scale. Yet the available silver in India hardly fell below 2000 lakhs—nearly three times the minimum at the most critical moment of the preceding year. The more than adequacy of their reserve at the busiest moment of the very busy season 1906–7 did not check, however, the impetuous activity of the Mints. During the summer of 1907, as in the summer of 1906, they continued to coin without waiting until the prosperity of the season 1907–8 was assured. In September 1907 their silver holdings in one form or another stood at the excessive figure of 3148 lakhs. This time they got what they deserved. The season of 1907–8 was a failure, and at the end of 1907 came the crisis in America. In place of there being a demand for new rupees, it was necessary to withdraw from circulation an immense volume of the old ones; and the sterling reserves, not the rupee reserves, were in danger of insufficiency. This leads us to the next chapter of the history.

7. The coinage policy of the Government of India from 1905 to 1907 suggests one obvious reflection. A succession of years, in which there is a heavy demand for currency, makes it less likely that the heavy demand will persist in the year following. The effects of heavy coinage are cumulative. The Indian authorities do not seem to have understood this. They were, to all appearances, influenced by the crude inductive argument that, because there was a heavy demand in 1905–6, it was likely that there would be an equally heavy demand in 1906–7; and, when there actually was a heavy demand in 1906–7, that this made it yet more likely that there would be a heavy demand in 1907–8. They framed their policy, that is to say, as though a community consumed currency with the same steady appetite with which some communities consume beer. In so far as the new currency is to satisfy the demands, not of hoarding, but of trade, it is hardly necessary to point out the fallacy. Moreover, even a superficial acquaintance with the currency history of India brings experience to the support of reason. Even when the rupee was worth no more than its bullion value, so that it was hoarded and melted much more than it is now, years

of unusually heavy coinage were nearly always followed by a reaction. India has taken her coinage in great gulps, and it need not have been difficult to see that the demand of 1905–7 was one of these.

8. The Government of India's silver policy during the early part of 1907 left them, therefore, in a somewhat worse position to meet the crisis which came at the end of the year, than need have been the case. But their sterling reserves were nevertheless fairly high. On September 1, 1907, they seem to have been, approximately, as follows:—

Gold—	
Currency Reserve in India	£4,100,000
Currency Reserve in London	6,200,000
	£10,300,000
Money at Short Notice—	
Gold Standard Reserve in London	£50,000
Cash Balances in London	5,150,000
	£5,200,000
Sterling Securities—	
In Currency Reserve	£1,300,000 [1]
In Gold Standard Reserve	14,100,000 [1]
	£15,400,000
Aggregate Sterling Reserves—	
Gold	£10,300,000
Money at Short Notice	5,200,000
Securities	15,400,000
	£30,900,000

Thus, to take a round figure, the crisis found the Secretary of State with about £31,000,000 in hand.

[1] Book value.

The storm was soon on him. By the end of October 1907 it had become plain that the Indian harvest would be a bad one, and the financial crisis in the United States was fast developing. On November 4 the Bank of England raised its rate to 6 per cent, and on November 7 (for the first time since 1873) to 7 per cent. On November 6 the Secretary of State could only manage to sell even 30 lakhs of rupees by allowing the rate to drop to the minimum figure of 1s. $3\frac{29}{32}$d. For several weeks following, at a time of year when the demand for Council Bills is usually strong, he sold none at all. But beyond withdrawing from the market he took no further steps for the support of exchange. This measure was inadequate to effect its purpose, and there is a good deal to be said for the view that he ought to have taken at once the more drastic steps for maintaining the gold value of the rupee which he had to take a few months later. However, it was a perplexing and unprecedented time for every one, and that it was some weeks before his advisers found their bearings is not to be wondered at.

So inadequate was his action that at first the fall in exchange was scarcely stayed at all. Tumbling day by day, it reached on November 25 the rate of $1/3\frac{11}{16}$. This is below the gold export point (from India), and it could not have fallen so low if the Government had made gold freely available in India. But, as can be seen from the preceding table, their Indian gold reserve was not large. Individuals were not permitted, therefore, to take out more than £10,000 at a time; and in this manner the gold dribbled slowly away over a period of a few months. It would probably have been of more use if it had been allowed to disappear in a week at the moment when it was most badly wanted.

In the meantime the Secretary of State, deprived of his usual source of income from the sale of Council Bills, was meeting his normal expenses from the gold portion of the Currency Reserve in London. But the Gold Standard Reserve, although about £1,000,000 worth of Consols was sold out in order to be ready for use in a more liquid form, was kept so far intact.

Thus matters went on until the end of December 1907, when the authorities nerved themselves, although the immediate necessity had temporarily disappeared through a slight strengthening of exchange, to take whatever drastic steps might be necessary to maintain the gold value of the rupee. It was announced that they would sell in India telegraphic transfers on London at a fixed rate. Before the need arose for acting on this announcement, it was changed into an offer to sell sterling bills on London at the fixed minimum rate of 1/3$\frac{29}{32}$.

By March 1908 the reserves of actual gold were nearly exhausted, but the securities and cash at short notice had not yet been trenched on. Early in April exchange was again weak, and the offer referred to above came into active operation. At first £500,000 a week, and later £1,000,000 a week of sterling bills on London were sold in India at $1/3\frac{29}{32}$. These were cashed in London from the proceeds of selling securities from the Gold Standard Reserve. By August 1908 about £8,000,000 of bills had been cashed in this way. At the beginning of September 1908 the sterling reserves, which I give for comparison with the amounts in September 1907 quoted above, were, approximately, as follows:—

Gold—	
Currency Reserve in India . . .	£150,000
Currency Reserve in London . .	1,850,000
	£2,000,000
Money at Short Notice—	
Gold Standard Reserve in London .	*nil.*
Cash Balances in London . . .	£1,850,000
	£1,850,000
Sterling Securities—	
In Currency Reserve	£1,300,000
In Gold Standard Reserve . . .	6,000,000
	£7,300,000
Aggregate Sterling Reserves—	
Gold	£2,000,000
Money at Short Notice	1,850,000
Securities	7,300,000
	£11,150,000

9. Thus the Secretary of State's sterling resources sank in the course of a year from about £31,000,000 to about £11,000,000. But these figures do not supply by themselves a complete explanation of the manner in which he had financed himself in London

during this period. Between September 1907 and September 1908 railway loans to the aggregate amount of about £12,500,000 and a loan of £2,000,000 for "general purposes"[1] were raised in sterling.[2] A large part of the former was required for the discharge of some previously existing railway debentures, and for the purchase in England of railway materials chargeable to capital account. In so far as the loan was used for these purposes it did not help the general position. But in so far as it was used for railway construction which could be paid for by rupees in India, it had the effect of increasing the Secretary of State's sterling resources by a corresponding amount. Altogether, during the period under review, the net assistance obtained by loans amounted, I think, to about £4,500,000; so that the total deterioration in the Secretary of State's position during the first year of the depression was not far short of £25,000,000.

After October 1908 the market still showed some hesitation. If the season had turned out poorly, it is clear that the Secretary of State must have had recourse to borrowing on a fairly heavy scale. In fact the harvest was satisfactory, and by December 1908 the demand for Council Bills was strong. It may

[1] A further loan of £2,500,000 for "general purposes" was incurred in December 1908.

[2] An unfunded debt of £6,000,000, which has been wiped off lately out of the proceeds of the opium windfall, was incurred by the issue of India Bills during this period.

be added to complete the story, that in August and September 1909 there was a short period of weakness when it was again necessary to offer sterling bills in Calcutta. Since that time India has enjoyed a period of very great prosperity, and, so far from the reserves being tested, it has been possible to build up the very strong position analysed above.

10. I have looked at the crisis so far from the point of view of its effect in depleting the sterling resources of the Secretary of State. To the authorities in India it presented its other face. There it was a question of how many rupees they would be able to withdraw from circulation. Unless there is a deficiency in the revenue from taxation, and apart from loans, the extent to which the Secretary of State can draw on sterling resources must exactly equal the extent to which the Government of India can withdraw rupees from circulation. For every transfer from the sterling branch of any of the reserves must be balanced by a corresponding transfer into the rupee branch. The amount of the sterling reserves is a measure of the ability of the authorities to withdraw rupees; and conversely, the volume of rupees which can be spared from the circulation (or from hoards) in bad times sets an upper limit to the extent to which they can be compelled to draw on their sterling reserves for the support of the currency.

Regarded from this standpoint, the facts were as follows:—By March 1908 nearly 115 million rupees had been withdrawn into the currency reserve by the release of gold, and by December 1908 the figure had risen to 154 million. Up to March 1908 it had not been necessary to take rupees into the Gold Standard Reserve; but by the end of November 1908 about 130 million rupees had been withdrawn in this way. There was also a small increase of rupees in that part of the Indian Cash Balances which is held in rupees and not in currency notes. Thus the active circulation was reduced altogether by about 285 million rupees (£19,000,000). This figure agrees closely enough with the figures we reached by studying the state of the sterling resources.

11. This completes the narrative of events up to the end of the crisis of 1908. I have given only such details as are relevant to my main topic—the adequacy of the reserves to fulfil their purpose.

12. Let us consider, first, the adequacy of the reserve of coined rupees. The governing facts of the situation are that every addition to the rupee reserve diminishes to an equivalent extent the amount available for the sterling reserve; that if the rupee reserve is insufficient, nothing worse can happen than some delay and inconvenience to merchants at a time of boom, whereas, if the sterling reserve is insufficient, a dangerous crisis may be aggravated to the pitch of panic; that at the last moment the rupee reserve can always be replenished with no very great delay from the resources of the sterling reserve, whereas the

reverse is not the case (the silver being not so saleable at a crisis as the gold is in a boom); and that, therefore, it is desirable to keep the rupee reserve at the lowest possible point consistent with probability and ordinary prudence. The practical information chiefly required for settling the proper policy is in regard to the ease with which new rupees can be supplied as they are wanted—as to how far, that is to say, the Government can safely pursue the policy of living from hand to mouth. This depends upon how fast silver can be bought by the Government without its submitting to extravagant charges, and how fast, in relation to the maximum rates of new demand so far experienced, the Indian Mints can turn the silver into rupees.

13. The Government of India's recent attempt to solve the first part of the problem unhappily involved its officers in a good deal of obloquy. The silver market is a very narrow one and can only be dealt in through the agency of one or other of a very small number of brokers. A ring of speculators lay waiting to force prices up as soon as the Government should appear as a buyer. Apart from the brokers who acted for the ring, there was only one firm in a position to buy large quantities of silver with the secrecy which was necessary if the speculators were to be defeated. Unfortunately the head of this firm was closely related by blood to the Parliamentary Under-Secretary of State. Two courses were open:

to buy openly and pay such extra price as the speculators might find themselves in a position to demand, or to risk charges of venality from any one who might have an interest in discrediting the Government—disappointed speculators, currency malcontents, or members of the political party in opposition. The officials, thinking (bureaucratically) more of the Indian Exchequer and the Indian taxpayer than of the House of Commons, chose, in fact, the second of the two alternatives—in a spirit, perhaps, of too great innocence, bred of long immunity from charges of personal corruption. It turned out that they had made insufficient allowance for the deep interest which the House of Commons takes in suggestions of personal scandal. The question of Indian currency became almost interesting. Members asked one another what the Gold Standard Reserve might be, and, when writers in the Press told them, were duly horrified to learn that it contained no gold. Closer inquiry elicited further facts unsuspected hitherto. It was discovered that a number of the most prominent members of the London Money Market were Jews, and that the Government of India's holdings of Consols had depreciated in market value since they were bought. But attention was specially concentrated on the fact that the cash balances held in London, after fluctuating considerably from time to time, had risen for a year past to an unusually high level, and had been lent out at low rates of interest to persons many of whom bore foreign names. How was the ordinary member of Parliament to be sure that some cosmopolitan syndicate of Jews was not fattening at the expense of the ryots of India, whose trustee he had often declared himself to be? Indian currency is too complicated a subject to be mastered at a moment's notice; and many persons, without paying much attention to random charges of corruption, felt, quite legitimately, that there was a great deal going on of which they had no conception, and that they would like to be fully satisfied for themselves, and not merely on the word of the officials, that everything was really in order. The situation in its fundamentals has arisen before, and will arise from time to time in the future so long as the relations of the House of Commons to India combine in a high degree responsibility and ignorance.

14. The circumstances themselves are of very transient importance, but they are likely to have some permanent effect on the particular question which we are now discussing. It will be too much to expect the officials to expose their personal reputations again to a suspicion, however ill-founded, even in the interests of the Indian Exchequer. Next time that the Government of India have to buy silver on a large scale, it is likely that they will do so publicly and pay such extra price as this policy involves. It is not worth a Government's while to risk its transactions falling into suspicion in

order to save half a million pounds. Assuming, therefore, that in future the Government will have to buy publicly, we have to consider whether it is likely to be cheaper for them to buy when the price of silver seems low, and hold stocks in hand, or to wait until the last moment and buy at whatever price is then ruling. I am inclined to think that the second of these two policies is the better —though it is plainly a matter on which it is not possible at present to see one's way clearly. It is outside the ordinary run of Government officials' duties to judge whether or not a given time is a good one at which to buy silver. The speculative business of estimating the future of silver is best left to experts in the matter, even though the price ultimately paid has to include some commission to them for their services or their foresight. In the second place the history of the recent speculative ring in silver, so far as it can be known to an outsider, does not suggest that such a transaction is a very easy or profitable thing to carry through, or that the speculators have had a sufficiently striking success to encourage similar attempts on a large scale in the future. I do not know with what profit the ring have emerged from the transaction; but the expense of carrying silver for a long period is great, and the rise in its price in the last two years, though substantial, has not been enough—so far as one can judge —to leave a surplus of profits at all commensurate with the great risks run. In the third place, it does not seem certain that the urgent demands for fresh coinage of rupees, to which India is subject from time to time, will be as frequent in the future as they have been in the immediate past. On the one hand the heavy coinages since 1900 are cumulative in their effect and render further coinages in the future less probable; and on the other hand an increased use (it is to be hoped) of other media of exchange will allow an urgent demand for currency to be met in other ways.

15. I do not think, therefore, that the Government need show a very long foresight lest they should have to buy silver dear. But when their stocks are falling low and there are apparently signs of demand in the *immediate* future, how long can coinage be delayed safely? To answer this we need to know the maximum rate of output of the Mints, and the maximum rate of absorption of new currency so far experienced.

16. The rates of absorption of rupees in various years have been given in the Table on p. 55. The maximum absorption in the October to December quarter was 11·39 lakhs in 1905-6, and the maximum in the January to March quarter was 2·68 lakhs in 1909-10. It has been estimated that the Indian Mints can turn out 2·25 lakhs of rupees per month without overtime, and 4·50 lakhs per month with overtime. There seems little reason, therefore, for over-anxiety lest the Government be caught short of rupees. If they were to start the busy season

with a surplus of 500 or 600 lakhs over what was considered a safe minimum, the reasonable demands of prudence would have been fully satisfied. The safe minimum in question must necessarily depend on circumstances, especially on the volume of the note issue and on the amount of gold held in India; it is impossible to suggest any figure which would be permanently suitable. I am dealing merely with the surplus over this minimum which, on the basis of experience, the Government might reasonably take pains to have in stock at the beginning of a busy season. The calculation refers throughout to their *aggregate* rupee resources in the Currency Reserve and Gold Standard Reserve combined.

17. We now come to the much more important question of the adequacy of the sterling reserves.

I do not think it has ever been thought out quite clearly for what precise purposes these reserves are held. The difficulty can be put shortly in this question, —Are they held purely as a currency reserve, or are they to fulfil also the purpose of a banking reserve? Is their only purpose, that is to say, to make certain that the Government will always be able to exchange for sterling such rupees and notes as may be presented to them, or are they also intended to ensure India's being able to meet her international obligations at a time of dangerous crisis? The two purposes are plainly not identical. If all bankers and merchants keep adequate reserves in rupees and notes, then it will be sufficient if the Government are always able to turn these rupees and notes into sterling. But if in a financial crisis the Indian Money Market as a whole is in fact unable to meet its international obligations without Government assistance, is it the Government's intention to stand calmly aside and permit (for example) a suspension of cash payments by the three Presidency Banks, or will they, if necessary, use their sterling reserves to give some support to the Indian Money Market *in extremis*?

If the Government's Reserve is held purely to support the currency, then the maximum volume of rupees and notes, which could, so far as one can anticipate, be spared from the circulation and tendered to the Government for exchange, sets an upper limit to the necessary amount of this Reserve. If, on the other hand, it is intended to act as a banking reserve and to ensure India's ability to meet her international obligations at all times, then its upper limit is set by the probable maximum amount of the adverse balance which could arise against India for immediate payment.

18. I will begin by discussing this question on the first hypothesis—that what the Government has been accumulating is intended to serve as a currency reserve only—and will return later to the problem of a reserve held for wider purposes, and of the possible magnitude of the balance of international indebtedness against India.

19. To estimate the demand that the reserves might have to meet merely in order to support the currency, the existing volume of currency is what we chiefly require to know. For this sets, or suggests, a limit to the maximum amount which can possibly be spared from the active circulation.

Attempts to estimate the rupee circulation of India have been the occasion of some very interesting calculations. For many years past (since 1875) an annual census of rupees has been taken by examining in each Government Treasury a bag containing 2000. This enabled Mr. F. C. Harrison, when he was Comptroller of Currency, to apply the Jevonian method very fully; and he was also able to corroborate his estimates by reference to the numbers of the older issues, 1835 and 1840 (*e.g.*), actually withdrawn from circulation on the occasions when the Mint recalled them. Mr. Harrison's results were checked by the labours of a later Comptroller of Currency, Mr. Adie, who applied to the same material two alternative methods of much greater technical complexity than Mr. Harrison's.[1]

Jevons's method is based on the assumptions that the proportions of coins issued at different dates found in the given samples roughly correspond to their proportions in the circulation at large, and that the numbers in circulation of the latest issues do not

[1] For details of the method applied in these various investigations see Appendices to Reports of Head Commissioner of Paper Currency, 1894, 1895, 1896, 1897, and 1900. See also Mr. Harrison's article on the "Rupee Census" in the *Economic Journal* for 1891.

much differ from the numbers issued from the Mint. In short, if we know the relative proportions of coins of 1860 and of 1912 in the circulation, and if we know, approximately, the absolute number of coins of 1912, we can calculate the absolute number still circulating of the coins of 1860. In applying this method to the Indian data, we are assuming that the proportions of rupees of each date found in the bags examined in a great number of scattered Government Treasuries are a fair sample of the proportions still in circulation throughout the country. In a country such as India, however, there may be great stagnancy in a part of the circulation, and the coins finding their way to the Government Treasuries may be a sample rather of the floating surplus of coinage, which has a relatively high velocity of circulation, than of the total stock, which includes semi-hoards passing from hand to hand comparatively seldom. Since these samples are likely, therefore, to contain an undue proportion of recent issues, estimates of the total circulation, which are based on them, may be expected to fall short of the truth rather than to exceed it. There is reason, also, for supposing that in some cases the officials charged with the duty of examining the samples did not always deal with them conscientiously. A tendency was noticed for the returns of one year to resemble those of the previous year more closely than they should, and not infrequently a batch of coins would be attributed to a year in which it is known that none were minted. Nevertheless the calculations of Mr. Harrison and Mr. Adie, and the data on which they are based, seem on the whole coherent, and bear, so far as one can judge, the marks of substantial accuracy.

A quite different method of estimating the circulation has been adopted by Mr. F. J. Atkinson.[1] His method is direct; and consists in a calculation or estimate of the additions to the currency and the losses from export, melting, etc., year by year, from 1831 when the modern coinage first began. Some of the items in the calculation are definitely known, but others, the amount annually melted, for example, are almost entirely a matter of guesswork. The fact that his calculations contain altogether a great number of separate guesses does not prevent his final result from being a guess too. For the period previous to the closing of the Mints some of his estimates for the amount melted seem very low, and this may possibly explain why his final results yield a much higher total for the circulation than those of Mr. Harrison and Mr. Adie. In recent times, *i.e.* since the closing of the Mints, and specially since the new equilibrium which was reached in 1900, Mr. Atkinson's method is much more satisfactory than for earlier years and, since the doubtful items are in these later years a far smaller proportion of the whole, much less likely to lead us wrong. For the earlier

[1] *Stat. Journ.* March 1897 and March 1903.

years, therefore, I am inclined to prefer Mr. Harrison's conclusions; but I think they can be brought up to date by a year-to-year method resembling Mr. Atkinson's. The increase in Mr. Atkinson's estimate during the 'nineties is due to the fact that, as his figures purport to exclude rupees in hoards, he must make large allowance for the coins from this source then entering into circulation.

The actual figures are as follows :—

ESTIMATE OF THE RUPEE CURRENCY IN CRORES (10,000,000) OF RUPEES

	Harrison.	Adie, 1st method.	Adie, 2nd method.	Atkinson.[1]
1881	about 115 (1881–1886)	108	...	135
1882		111	108	133
1883		113	110	136
1884		106	107	136
1885		104	105	139
1886		106	110	145
1887	...	109	108	148
1888	120	106	106	152
1889	...	112	112	154
1890	...	121	115	159
1891	...	121	116	166
1892	125	129	121	167
1893	128	132	130	173
1894	...	129	126	176
1895	...	128	127	169
1896	...	121	120	172
1897	...	116	116	178
1898	120	118	113	183
1899	...	118	112	178
1900	...	...	...	177
1901	...	...	...	189

[1] Of Mr. Atkinson's two separate calculations, made in 1897 and 1903, I have taken the latter. His calculation explicitly excludes rupees in hoards, currency reserves, and Government balances; and is not, therefore, entirely comparable with the others. If it were, the excess would be considerably greater than it actually appears above.

20. These are the *data*. It is very difficult to estimate the extent to which rupees may have emerged from hoards during the period which succeeded the closing of the Mints. Mr. Atkinson's figures suggest that rupees from this source not only made good the natural wastage in the active circulation but actually brought about a large increase in it. Judging from the course of prices, I think he must have made an excessive allowance under this head. The figures of Mr. Harrison and Mr. Adie, on the other hand (which refer to the *total* circulation), point to a more moderate influx out of hoards into current use. I propose to take a middle course, nearer, however, to Mr. Harrison than to Mr. Atkinson, and to assume a *public* circulation in 1900 (*i.e.*, excluding rupees in the Currency Reserve and Government Balances) of 120 crores of rupees. This estimate is probably near enough to the truth for our purpose. If it is incorrect, I think it is more likely to be an underestimate than an overestimate.

Starting from this assumption, I have worked out the details given in the following table as a guide to the probable circulation at the present time. By *public* circulation, whether of rupees or notes, I mean the whole circulation not in the hands of the Government—*i.e.*, including that in the hands of the banks. I am primarily concerned with the circulation of rupees; but the public circulation of notes has been added in the last column but one, as it is useful to know at the same time the *total* public circulation of currency.

CURRENCY IN LAKHS OF RUPEES

Financial Year, April 1–March 31.	Public Circulation of Rupees on April 1.	New Coinage less Recoinage[1] etc.[2]	Rupees released from Currency, Gold Exchange Standard, and Treasury Reserves.	Net[3] Export.	Public Circulation of Rupees on March 31.[4]	Public Circulation of Notes on March 31.	Total Currency in the hands of the Public on March 31.[4]
1900–1901	120,00	+13,60	− 4,66	− 35	=128,59	+23,79	=152,38
1901–1902	128,59	+ 2,04	− 2,72	− 1,42	=126,49	+24,24	=150,73
1902–1903	126,49	+ 60	− 58	− 2,23	=124,28	+28,87	=153,15
1903–1904	124,28	+11,42	− 45	+ 40	=135,65	+31,54	=167,19
1904–1905	135,65	+ 6,88	+ 55	− 61	=142,47	+33,73	=176,20
1905–1906	142,47	+16,11	− 2,11	− 78	=155,69	+37,90	=193,59
1906–1907	155,69	+22,88	− 4,88	− 1,28	=172,41	+41,20	=213,61
1907–1908	172,41	+15,48	−11,56	− 41	=175,92	+38,65	=214,57
1908–1909	175,92	+ 2	−14,90	− 29	=160,75	+39,23	=199,98
1909–1910	160,75	+ 8	+13,14	− 1,39	=172,42	+46,51	=218,93
1910–1911	172,42	− 42	+ 3,76	− 1,72	=174,04	+45,68	=219,72
1911–1912	174,04	− 7	+11,61	− 1,13	=184,41	+53,24	=237,65
1912–1913	184,41						

[1] This column is derived from the figures given by the Currency Department, and the total of net coinage issued in individual years differs somewhat from the total amount minted as stated in the Mint Statistics.

[2] In one or two of the earlier years deduction is made on account of an appreciable sum in rupees paid out to native states. This deduction is in accordance with the practice of the reports of the Currency Department.

[3] For Bahrein Islands, Ceylon, Arabia, Mauritius, and East African Coast.

[4] Not allowing for natural wastage of rupees (see below).

This calculation makes no allowance for the general wastage through loss and various causes, or for the steady drain of rupees across the land frontiers. This last item is probably considerable and is not adequately accounted for in the trade returns. The recorded statistics of trade overland show a large annual balance against India, which is probably met by an unrecorded export of gold, silver bullion, and rupees. In the case of Nepal, for example, the recorded statistics show a considerable net balance of imports of treasure *into* India; and in the case of Tibet, Afghanistan and, in fact, all the land frontiers, the official statistics of the export of treasure do not tally with what we know of the circulation of the rupee beyond the frontiers. Taking all these causes of loss together, I do not think we should overestimate the wastage of rupees from the circulation in placing it between half a crore and a crore annually. For the twelve years 1900 to 1912, therefore, I propose to make an aggregate deduction of 941 lakhs.

This leaves us with a public circulation of 175 crores of rupees (£116,500,000) on March 31, 1912, and a total public circulation, including notes, of 228 crores[1] (£152,000,000), being an increase since 1900 of 46 per cent in the rupee circulation and of 58 per cent in the total circulation. If Mr. Atkinson's estimate of the circulation in 1900 is nearer the truth than Mr. Harrison's, then the public rupee circulation in 1912 may have been as much as 200 crores. In the course of 1912 there was a good deal of fresh coinage, of which, at the time of writing, accurate statistics are not yet available. For our present purpose it will be quite sufficiently cautious to think of the public rupee and note circulation together as amounting to not more than 250 crores.

21. How much of this could possibly be spared from circulation at a time of crisis? In 1908 the

[1] This represents a *per capita* circulation of between Rs. 7 and Rs. 8.

rupee circulation fell (at its lowest point) by somewhat less than 30 crores, or less than 20 per cent of the estimated rupee circulation at that time. The note circulation (see p. 55) fell much less seriously. It does not seem to me likely that the Government could be called on at the present time to redeem more than 25 per cent of the total circulation (notes and rupees together), or, on the basis of the foregoing calculations, 60 crores (say) of rupees (£40,000,000). If the Government were to keep in one way or another a reserve of this amount for purely currency purposes, I think they would have done as much as reasonable prudence could require. I do not say that it is impossible that they should be called on to redeem a greater amount than this. But it would be extravagant to maintain a reserve adequate for all conceivable emergencies, since there is a further resort of which use might fairly be made without great reluctance. Unless the London Money Market has collapsed as well as the Indian, it is always open to the Secretary of State to borrow by means of India Bills. There would be nothing shameful in this—though possibly some expense. But the expense, even if the Secretary of State had to pay a rate of interest appropriate to Turkey or China, would be much less than the expense of maintaining a very great reserve against unlikely emergencies.[1]

[1] In 1899, the Government of India contemplated the possibility of a loan. See their despatch of August 24, 1899 (H. of C. 495 of 1913, p. 13):—"If India were afflicted with famine or other adverse circumstances in the earlier

22. So much for the proper magnitude of the Reserve, regarded as a Currency Reserve. The question of its use as a Banking Reserve raises two problems—a problem of policy and a problem of statistics. Ought the Government to allow its Reserve to be used as a Banking Reserve? If so, how large ought this Reserve to be? Let us consider policy first.

23. There are three kinds of crises by which the Indian Money Market might be assailed—a purely internal crisis, in which the banks have difficulty in meeting a run on them by their Indian depositors; a purely external crisis, in which India owes, and is called on to pay, large sums in the London Market, but is free from serious banking trouble at home; and a general crisis, in which the features of an internal and an external crisis are combined.

A purely internal crisis of the first kind might require assistance from the resources of Government, but would involve no claims on their sterling resources specifically, as distinguished from their rupee resources. The trouble would probably begin with a boom of the usual type, heavy commitments on the part of the banks, large importations of foreign goods, and (in the future) a good deal of internal

years of our new currency, and before an adequate reserve had accumulated, circumstances might arise in which borrowing to maintain the standard would become an absolute necessity. We should have preferred to have been armed against such a contingency . . . not by actual borrowing but by obtaining power to borrow. . . . We have learnt with satisfaction . . . that your lordship has stated in the House of Commons that borrowing would be resorted to if it should prove to be necessary."

company promoting. If, early in the autumn, a serious failure of the monsoon became apparent, a widespread suspension on the part of the numerous bubble banks, which have been springing up lately all over India,[1] would be a probable consequence. Indian depositors generally might take alarm and hoard money in their own houses on a large scale. Exchange Banks have such large deposits in India and so little cash there[2] that they would probably require to import funds from London as fast as possible. The Indian Joint Stock Banks, however, are now so important that the part played by the Exchange Banks might not be adequate to save the situation. The Government would then be called on to make advances to the Presidency Banks. This has happened from time to time in the past, the last occasion being in April 1898, when the Bank of Bombay, whose bank rate was then at 13 per cent, asked the Government for an advance of 25 lakhs.[3]

This raises the first question of policy—whether the Government should help the bankers' reserves on an occasion of internal crisis by making rupee advances to them. But it is hardly relevant to the question of the Government's *sterling* resources; and, unless the Government Savings Banks were to be in trouble at the same time, it is not likely that

[1] See Chap. VII. [2] See p. 215.

[3] The Government was on the point of sanctioning this advance when the urgent necessity for it came to an end, and the advance was not actually made.

there would be any difficulty in helping the bankers, if it were thought right to do so.

A crisis of the second kind, due to general depression or bad harvests, in which India has to meet a heavy adverse balance in London, provided that, as in 1907, it is not accompanied by internal banking difficulties of the kind just described, causes, it is true, a drain on the Government's sterling resources through the necessity of providing remittance on London, but only in proportion to the volume of notes and rupees which are brought to the Government for encashment or in payment of sterling drafts.

At first, therefore, in such a case, there is no question of the Government's using its reserves otherwise than as currency reserves; and the banks will have plenty of notes and rupees with which to buy the Government's sterling drafts. Only if the depression is very prolonged, and one bad harvest follows another, is the need likely to arise for sterling advances from Government, otherwise than against a corresponding face value of notes and rupees.

It is not very improbable, however, that in the future there might be a general crisis of the third kind—a heavy adverse balance against India, and an internal banking crisis at the same time. It is in these circumstances that the most difficult question of policy arises. The Indian Money Market would need to remit funds to London, but, on account of the internal banking crisis and an outbreak of hoarding amongst depositors, would not have even rupee resources with which to do it. Consequently the Government's offer to sell sterling drafts in Calcutta, or to release gold from the Currency Reserve would not meet the case. If general distrust of banking was widely spread, and notes, gold, and rupees were being hoarded in the old-fashioned way on a large scale, the banks would not be able to put their hands on sufficient cash resources of any kind to enable them to pay for the Government's drafts on a scale adequate to their necessities. The position would be that the Indian Money Market was on the verge of general insolvency with the Presidency Bank Rates at (say) 12 per cent, and that the Indian Government had (say) £40,000,000 sterling resources in hand with demands on only a modest scale for the encashment of notes and rupees. The Government would be vehemently urged to save the situation by making sterling advances, not simply in exchange for notes or rupees, but on some other non-monetary security.

24. We now have the possibilities before us. If in any of these sets of circumstances the Government were faced with demands for advances either in rupees or sterling, what line would it be proper to take?

On the one hand the policy of advances may introduce into the Indian Money Market a serious element of weakness,—an element, perhaps, inseparable from a system where there is no central banking authority and where the currency authority stands, normally, outside the money market. It is not the business of the Government to hold any of the reserves which the bankers ought to hold. But if the Government does, in fact, for another purpose hold large reserves in its hands, and if it is believed that it will in case of extreme necessity come to the market's rescue, the bankers may tend to keep somewhat lower reserves than they ought, and than they otherwise would. We have over again the situation which has long existed, to its detriment, in the United States. There, as in India, the Government, with immense currency reserves of gold, is normally aloof from the money market. There also they have no central banking authority. The expectation that the Government will bring some of its gold to the rescue in extreme circumstances, has always been said to exert an enervating influence on the banks themselves in the matter of the precautions they take for times of crisis. The ultimate solution probably lies in the establishment of a Central Bank for India which shall be the Government Bank and shall hold the banking and currency reserves at the same time.[1]

In the meantime, in spite of this consideration, the Government will not, I think be able to resist

[1] I will recur to this proposal in Chapter VII.

the pressure on them in a crisis to come to the assistance of the market. Indeed, I do not know that they ought to resist it. It would be absurd to have large reserves in hand, and not to use them to avert a general calamity. The awkwardness of the situation is intrinsic, and cannot be avoided so long as the present divorce is maintained between the banking and the currency authorities. The plans of the Government ought, therefore, to be laid accordingly.

25. If there is force in this contention, and unless the Government of India have definitely made up their minds that their sterling reserves are to be used in no circumstances except for the support of exchange and of the sterling value of their currency, it is important to understand that immediate action is essential, and that to delay action for a few weeks may be fatal. I would emphatically apply to India the well-known doctrine which the powerful advocacy of Mr. Bagehot raised in England, many years ago, to an impregnable position in the unwritten constitution of this country—the doctrine, namely, that in a time of panic the reserves of the Bank of England must, at a suitably high rate, be placed at the disposal of the public without stint and without delay. There is a danger that the matter may not be thought out until, quite suddenly, the financial crisis comes, and that then, while the decision is being taken and the best advice sought, an inadvertent

delay will intervene. If there were signs of a general banking crisis in India, and particularly if the position of the Exchange Banks were weakening in England, I am inclined to think that it would be a wise policy on the part of Government to make an immediate announcement that they would place up to (say) £10,000,000 at the disposal of the Presidency Banks (or other approved borrowers) at a rate of (say) 10 per cent. If this action stayed, as it well might, the run on the banks in India, and the difficulties of the Exchange Banks in raising temporary loans in London, the Government might with a very moderate loss of funds (the mere announcement that they were available being sufficient) find itself in a far more favourable position for dealing with the subsequent depression; whereas after a delay a similar announcement might eventually be forced upon them, and if the panic had then gained impetus, the £10,000,000 quickly lapt up.

26. Two points connected with the above may be emphasised before we pass on to the statistical problem. In the first place, in the event of a *financial* crisis, accompanied by numerous bank failures, I do not think it likely that the Government would be overwhelmed with demands for the encashment in sterling of notes and rupees. It would be much more in accordance with what we know of similar crises elsewhere to expect hoarding on a large scale, rather than a diminished demand for currency and an ability to

export it. In this matter the experience of 1907–8, when the monetary position in India was easy throughout, may prove, I think, misleading. During the eventful weeks in November 1907, when the Bank of England rate stood at 7 per cent, the Bank of Bengal rate did not rise above 6 per cent.[1] No tendency whatever was apparent for there to be withdrawals of money from the banks in India, or for hoarding to reassert itself amongst the class which is learning to bank. On the other hand, the comparative failure of the crops left financiers with considerable rupee funds in their hands which they could not use. The banks had, therefore, no special difficulty in putting their hands on rupees and notes, and the only problem was for the Government to turn these into sterling. The easiness of the internal money market at that time and the total absence of banking trouble have produced the impression that there will be plenty of rupee funds available at a crisis, and that the only question will be as to whether the Government can turn these into sterling. The great development of Indian Joint Stock Banking since that time on not perfectly sound lines makes it doubtful whether bank troubles will be absent in an equal degree on the next occasion of difficulty.

[1] For the movements of the Indian bank-rate in the autumn and spring of 1907–8, see the chart appended to Chap. VIII. Eventually, on January 16, 1908, the Bengal rate did rise to 9 per cent (the Bombay rate did not rise to this level until February 7); but this is not very abnormal in the winter, and the average rate for money in 1907–8 was lower than in the corresponding season of the two busy years 1905–6 and 1906–7.

There is no one now living in England within whose memory hoarding has been a normal thing. But in countries where the tradition is but lately dead or still lingers, it is apt to revive with astonishing vitality at the least sign of danger. The extent to which the people resorted to hoarding in France, Germany, and Austria (especially in the latter country) during the Balkan War was very remarkable, and has exhibited a danger to which the banking systems of those countries are still subject, although some had begun to forget it. If this is the case in European countries, there cannot be much doubt as to what would happen in India. Some banking failures, a hint of political trouble,—and the old habits will come back, whatever progress banking may seem to have made in a time of prosperity

But, secondly, assuming a sharp financial crisis to be accompanied by increased hoarding, it would plainly be better if it were a hoarding of rupees and notes rather than of gold. It is not impossible that this might be the case. A trust in the Government's capacity to meet its obligations will persist some time after all confidence in private institutions has been dissolved. In Austria, for example, the hoarding was not so much of gold or silver as of notes. I believe that in some parts of India, especially in those where gold has made relatively little progress, hoards are sometimes held already to a fair extent in notes. I know, for example, a very conservative Brahmin family, small landowners in Eastern Bengal, where this is the case. Once a week the head of the family will retire privately to a corner of the roof of the house, take out the little hoard of notes with ritual care, count and check them, dust each with a feather brush, and lay them out in the sun to air and to recover from any trace of damp. If a note shows signs of age or wear, it is taken to the nearest currency office and changed for a new one. In troubled times such a family would hoard more notes or silver, not gold. This, however, is no more than an illustration of the point I have already dwelt on and emphasised—the manner in which any increase in the popularity of gold diminishes the stability of the currency.

27. Returning from these digressions, I conclude that the Government will not be able in practice to restrict its responsibility to the currency, and may have to take a part in moderating the consequences of rash or unfortunate banking, and in meeting an adverse balance of indebtedness. This conclusion brings us to the statistical problem. Is the £40,000,000, which I put forward as a safe maximum for the reserves, so far as the convertibility of the currency is concerned, still adequate when the possible magnitude of India's adverse balance of indebtedness is our test of sufficiency?

This problem is even less capable than the former of exact solution. The *variable* elements in India's international balance-sheet are chiefly (i.) the excess of exports over imports, including treasure, *i.e.*, the trade balance; (ii.) the amount of *new* fixed capital lent to India by European capitalists; and (iii.) the amount of short-period loans afforded to India by the European Money Market.

We require to know the magnitude of possible *variation* in these items, rather than the absolute amount of the various annual payments which India has to make, in order to gauge the possible balance of indebtedness against her. The greatest stress is commonly placed on the first of them—the trade balance. But in the normal state of affairs receipts and payments only balance after account has been taken of capital transactions; and if a certain amount of new capital has been flowing in every year, a slackening of this flow affects the balance as adversely as a reduction in the volume of exports affects it. In 1907–8 the adverse balance of indebtedness was largely due to a change in the trade balance;—on the one hand, goods ordered during the boom continued to pour into Bombay for some weeks after they had become unsaleable, thus continuing for a time a large supply of bills on India, while, on the other hand, the failure of the monsoon and consequent anticipations of a scanty harvest cut off a considerable part of the normal supply of trade bills on London. But even on this occasion the adverse balance arose to a considerable extent out of changes in capital transactions under items (ii.) and (iii.). The acute stringency in the international money markets, occasioned by the position in America, made it necessary for Exchange Banks and others to reduce below their normal level their short-period borrowings (direct or indirect) in London for use in India; and this stringency also caused the flow of new investment to India to fall short of its usual volume.

Thus, of the adverse balance of some £25,000,000 which had to be met between September 1907 and September 1908, perhaps £18,000,000 was due to a change in the trade balance and £7,000,000 to a diminution of new capital transactions and to the non-renewal of some short-period loans.[1] It is not easy, however, to argue from the experience of 1907–8 as to what will happen in the future. The volume of trade has expanded very greatly since that time,[2] and the absolute variation in the favourable balance between good years and bad is likely to be correspondingly greater. In addition, the growth of banking in the intervening period has been on a very great scale; and there is, therefore, greater room for disturbance in the short-period loan market. If, moreover, the internal banking position in India is as weak as in Chapter VII. I make it out to be, a serious breakdown there

[1] For a fuller discussion of this question in relation to the events of 1907–8, see my article on "Recent Economic Events in India" in the *Economic Journal*, March 1909.

[2] Aggregate exports of Indian produce and manufactures: 1906–7, £115,625,135; 1911–12, £147,818,000.

may embarrass the Exchange Banks in London, however intrinsically sound the position of these Banks may really be, in their efforts to assist the Indian market.

28. These are the relevant considerations. But any conclusion as to the possible magnitude of the adverse balance at which one can arrive on the basis of them is little better than a guess. I will give my guess for what it is worth. I think the £40,000,000, which I have fixed as the maximum figure of what is required for the redemption in sterling of such notes and rupees as may be presented, is more than sufficient to meet the adverse balance that is at all likely to emerge in any single year. But I do not think it certain that this sum would be adequate to the necessities of two successive bad years. On the other hand, it is necessary to bear in mind that by the second bad year there would have been time for a very great reduction in the volume of imports, on account of the greatly reduced purchasing power of the people, and that this might go a long way towards righting the balance; also that, if there was a considerable liquidation of short-period loans in the first year, it would not be necessary to repeat this to anything like the same extent in the second year. In short, the *natural* forces tending towards equilibrium would begin in the second year to show themselves more strongly. Nor is it necessary to accumulate reserves in advance for every eventuality. Two bad years in

succession are not very likely; and, if they do come, the Secretary of State will have ample time to make his arrangements for borrowing.

I think it a sufficient concession, therefore, if the £40,000,000 be given as the proper limit, not as before of the aggregate sterling resources of all kinds, but of the Gold Standard Reserve and the sterling branch of the Paper Currency Reserve (*i.e.* excluding the Cash Balances).

In a country such as India, where all available resources are required for capital expansion, and where it is not sound or humane policy to burden the present overmuch for the sake of the future, it is nearly as important to avoid extravagance in the reserve policy as to avoid undue parsimony. As the rupee and note circulation is increased, the proportion of reserves ought to grow, of course, *pari passu*. But in existing circumstances to hold much more than £40,000,000 in sterling in the Gold Standard Reserve and the Paper Currency Reserve together would border on extravagance. If the reserves were somewhat lower than this, I do not think it would necessarily be blameworthy to leave them so, provided it would prove a very burdensome thing to raise them. For the expedient of a loan is always available.[1] My conclusion, rather, is that the reserves should be allowed to reach some such figure as this

[1] The Government of India stands in a particularly strong position in this respect, because few countries have so good a market for their loans at a foreign centre as India has.

by the natural processes of growth, before sums are diverted from them to other purposes.

A very few years ago hopes of reaching so secure a position as this would have seemed chimerical. But the details given on p. 131 show that in December 1912 the sterling reserves already amounted to somewhat more than this. It is not yet clear, however, that their present amount is normal. If it turns out to be so, then a position of adequate strength has been attained already. But the form in which these reserves are held is open to much criticism, and this must be my next topic.

29. The criticisms which have had most popular vogue have been mainly directed against the absolute amount of the Gold Standard Reserve, against the investment of a large part of this reserve in securities, and against the maintenance in London of some part of the gold in the Currency Reserve.

In regard to the amount of the Gold Standard Reserve, Lord Curzon, in 1904, was inclined to think that £10,000,000 would be a proper figure. In 1905 Sir E. Law, the Financial Member of the Viceroy's Council, suggested £20,000,000. In 1906 Sir E. Baker thought £20,000,000 a suitable minimum. More recently, in 1912, £25,000,000 is the amount which responsible officials have announced that they are aiming at. Sir E. Law and Sir E. Baker both based their estimates on the amount which the Secretary of State would require for his Home

Charges if he had to curtail his drawings of Council Bills by one-third or one-half for a considerable period. I do not think that this is the most useful point of view from which to approach the question, or that the proper magnitude of the Gold Standard Reserve can be discussed without reference to the magnitude of the other reserves.

30. The other two criticisms quoted above lead on to the general question of how the sterling resources should be held and how they should be divided between the several Reserves. The second of these questions is mainly a matter of book-keeping, but has nevertheless some importance. The Government of India's present system has no logical basis, is exceedingly difficult to understand, and has often led, in consequence, to a good deal of misunderstanding. The ideal system should be as simple and logical as is compatible with leaving the authorities a free hand to shift and adjust as the necessities of the moment may require. The present system is the outcome partly of historical origins, partly of the authorities' not having allowed themselves by law a perfectly free hand. The much criticised practice, for example, of holding six crores of coined rupees in the Gold Standard Reserve is probably due to the provision by which that portion of the Currency Reserve, which is held in London, can be held only in gold. If rupees have to be released hurriedly from the silver portion of the Gold Standard Reserve in India, the authorities

have a completely free hand as to the form in which they make the corresponding addition to their sterling reserves in London; whereas, if they are released from the Currency Reserve, the corresponding transference in London must be made wholly in gold coin—a course which may sometimes be exceedingly inconvenient at the moment.

31. If the authorities allowed themselves more latitude as to the manner in which the Currency Reserve might be held, it would be a mere book-keeping transaction to transfer to this reserve the rupees now held in silver in the Gold Standard Reserve and to replace them by a corresponding transfer of gold; but such an arrangement would be more logical and easier to understand.

32. I think, therefore, that there might be considerable advantages in the adoption of some general scheme for the reserves such as the following:—

(1) While it would be legal to hold the Gold Standard Reserve in *any* form—gold, securities, bills of exchange, loans, or rupees—it should be normal in good times to hold, say, £11,000,000 in sterling securities and the rest in gold either in London or India, but preferably in London.

(2) Power should be taken to invest a larger amount of the Currency Reserve than at present (say £7,500,000 sterling securities in addition to the rupee securities instead of £2,500,000 as at present), and to hold a prescribed maximum proportion (say one-

third) of it in bills of exchange or on loan at short notice either in India or London.

All this, after the necessary change of law, could be effected by a change in book-keeping; and in December 1912 the account would have stood as follows (compare the actual state of affairs as given on p. 131):—

Gold—	
Gold Standard Reserve in London	£7,500,000
Gold Standard Reserve in India	2,500,000
Currency Reserve in India	15,000,000
	£25,000,000
Money at Short Notice—	
Currency Reserve in London	£1,000,000
Cash Balances in London	7,500,000
	£8,500,000
Sterling Securities—	
Currency Reserve	£7,500,000
Gold Standard Reserve	11,000,000
	£18,500,000
Rupees—	
Currency Reserve	£13,750,000

33. Some changes of substance might be added to these changes in book-keeping and are naturally suggested by them. There is, first, the question whether the gold portion of the reserves ought to be held in India or in London. Readers of Chapter IV. will know that there are, in my opinion, no advantages in keeping gold in India, and that such a policy involves a direct money loss through the cost of originally

carrying the gold to India and the cost of bringing it back again to London when, at a later date, it is required to support exchange. But Indian opinion views with suspicion the holding in London of the greater part of India's gold reserve, and this opinion, though ill-founded, is likely to persist for some time to come. The amount of expense involved in keeping gold in the Indian reserves is, in relation to the issues involved, not great; and it might be well worth while to incur it in order to avoid the currency system's falling under a suspicion, however ill-founded. It might be a satisfactory compromise, therefore, if, as a normal practice (but not as a legal requirement), the gold in the Gold Standard Reserve were held "ear-marked" at the Bank of England, but the gold in the Currency Reserve retained in India. It may be added that the authorities seem, in fact, to be moving somewhat in this direction; for it is understood to be their intention to accumulate £5,000,000 in gold "ear-marked" for the Gold Standard Reserve.

If, however, a large part of the gold be held in India, it is of the utmost importance, in the event of a crisis, that the gold should be shipped by the Government to London and sterling drafts on London sold against it, or, if it were released in India, that the banks only should be allowed to get it, and on an undertaking to export it. Otherwise, if it were made freely available in India, a part might be lost and wasted (so far as the support of exchange is concerned) in hoards.

34. The suspicion which is felt with regard to the holding of Indian gold in London is exceedingly natural, and can be completely dissipated only by a fuller knowledge of the currency system and of the mechanism of the foreign exchanges, than the generality is likely to possess. It is natural to think that this gold is more at the disposal of the London Money Market than it would be if it were in India, and that the Secretary of State, under corrupt or interested pressure, can easily place it at the disposal of London financiers. Apart from the question how far the Secretary of State is really open to such pressure, it may be doubted whether he is likely to be exposed to it, because at a time of real stringency it will prove easy, I believe, for the London Market to get hold of some part of the Indian Gold, whether held in London or in India, by perfectly legitimate means. India is normally in the position of owing London money; this debt is discharged partly by the consignment of goods, partly by the renewal at frequent intervals of short loans or credits made by the London Market to the Indian Market on bills of exchange or through the Exchange Banks, and partly by new permanent loans. If there is great stringency in the London Market and London is in urgent need of funds, the use of the last two methods can be so much restricted that India can be practically forced

to pay what is owing in gold. It is, in fact, precisely because she is open to this pressure that it is necessary for a considerable gold reserve to be kept. So long, therefore, as the gold is freely available either in India or in London for the support of exchange, it is unlikely that it can be withheld from the London Money Market if this Market really wants it. If it is in London, India will be able, by the sale of telegraphic sterling transfers in Calcutta, to discharge her due obligations cheaply and without delay; if it is in Calcutta, additional charges and a loss of time must be incurred.

A feeling of jealousy on a country's part, lest some other country should have a lien on its gold reserve, is frequently liable to arise at the present time, but is essentially opposed in spirit to the whole purpose and meaning of keeping gold reserves at all. Gold reserves are meant to be used in times of difficulty, and for the discharge of pressing obligations. It is absurd for a man with a large balance at his bank to default to his creditors, because a feeling of jealousy, in regard to any one in whose favour he draws a cheque, prevents him from ever drawing one. Mr. Bagehot certainly did England a great service in dissipating from the minds of her financiers this primitive prejudice;—for wonderfully few other countries have yet learnt that gold reserves, although no doubt they serve some purpose when they are held for show only, exist to much better purpose if they are held for use also.

Vague stirrings of the original sin of mercantilism always inherent in the mind of the natural man and urging him to regard gold as beyond everything essential wealth; jealousy of the too powerful magnates of the London Money Market obtaining what should belong to India's Market for their own purposes; jealousy of the Secretary of State seeming, like a man who invests abroad, to seek in this way an independence of India in case of trouble; jealousy of Great Britain, who might use or regard India's "ear-marked" gold as her own war-chest;—all combine to make a powerful, natural, and yet unfounded prejudice which it is exceedingly difficult to combat. Nothing is commoner than to read incitements against malevolent financiers who would seek to deprive India of her "fair share" of the world's new gold. India must be allowed, I suppose, to hug her sterile favourite. In spite of the notorious fact that the Bank of England holds less gold than the Central Bank of any other first-class Power,—far less even than the Caja of the Argentine,—the belief will continue that the amount of gold a country holds at home, rather than the degree of promptness and certainty with which at all times it can meet its international engagements, is the measure of its financial strength.

35. What other changes of substance might be made usefully? By far the most important is connected with the proposed power to make advances from the Currency Reserve on bills of exchange and

other approved security, as briefly described in Chapter III.

The policy pursued during 1912 of holding large cash balances in London and of lending them out in the London Market provoked widespread criticism both in India and at home. The line of thought underlying this criticism appears to me to be entirely reasonable. If the Government of India hold in London a penny more than is required to establish the stability of their financial system, they are certainly diverting resources from India, where they are greatly required, to the detriment of India's own trade. I do not think, however, that the authorities are in fact open to any serious blame up to the present time. The holding of such large balances in London has not been part of a permanent policy, and was due in 1912 to a combination of circumstances which could not easily have been foreseen. And further, the Government have not until quite lately held more sterling resources altogether than have been required for the stability of the system. Public feeling points, nevertheless, in the direction of what, in the future, will be the right policy. If I am right in thinking that about £40,000,000 in the sterling Reserves is in present circumstances adequate, further accumulations in the hands of Government ought to be put at the disposal of the Indian Money Market and not converted into sterling. At present there is no machinery for doing this; and the absence of the appropriate arrangements constitutes a serious gap in the country's financial system. What would be thought in France or Germany, or in any other European country, if an expansion of the note issue could not be made against the discount of home bills, but only against a corresponding deposit in cash cent per cent? Yet this is the position in India. The Government (apart from their deposits in the Presidency Banks, which will be dealt with later on) have no choice between allowing the funds which accumulate in their hands to lie absolutely idle in India and transferring them to London to earn a low rate of interest there.

If the use of notes continues to increase, and if £40,000,000 is an adequate figure for the sterling Reserves, a considerable sum may soon be available in India from the funds of the Paper Currency Reserve. Every addition, moreover, to the Gold Standard Reserve reduces to some extent the need for holding large amounts of sterling in the Paper Currency Reserve. Great advantages may be obtained if the surplus funds in the Paper Currency Reserve be used, not as a permanent or quasi-permanent loan to Indian traders, but to provide *elasticity* in the seasonal supply of currency and to make possible the increase in the stock of purchasing power in the form of money which is *temporarily* required in the busy season, without having to raise it in London. *Per-*

manent additions to the currency must be obtained in the future as they are at present. But *temporary* additions, due to seasonal demand, ought to be provided by a suitable organisation of credit money in India herself.

The advances from the Currency Reserve, therefore, must be made at a fairly high rate of interest and for periods not exceeding three months; and they should be so arranged that the Government would regain possession of its funds and the advances be reduced to *nil* in each slack season. Thus the Government would begin each busy season with their funds intact; and they would not lend until the success of the season was assured, and it was plain that the general position warranted it. The advances would be made in notes or rupees, according to the demand. These prosperity advances, therefore, are to be sharply distinguished from the adversity advances, discussed on pp. 160-163, which would be made in sterling drafts, and which would be governed by wholly different considerations.

36. There remains for discussion the question of the Government's Cash Balances.[1] I will begin with the method of managing that part of them which is held in India. It will be useful to know in what way this method has grown up.[2]

When, in 1862, the right of note issue was taken away from the Presidency Banks, they were given as

[1] In continuation of what has been said in § 4.

[2] See Brunyate, *loc. cit.* chap. vii., from which the greater part of what follows is summarised.

part recompense the use of the whole of that part of the Government balances which would otherwise have been received at the General Treasury, or at places where the Banks had branches, provided that sums in excess of a prescribed amount (70 lakhs in the case of the Bank of Bengal), if not held in cash, should be invested in Government paper and other authorised securities. Difficulties very soon arose (in 1863) through the Government's requiring the use of its funds at a time when the Bank of Bengal could only sell out the securities in which it had invested them at a considerable loss. The system of virtually compelling the Banks to lock up the Government funds in securities, not easily saleable at all times, was plainly vicious, and in 1866 a new arrangement was made by which the Banks were permitted to use the whole of the balances, placed with them for the time being, for banking purposes. This seems to have worked satisfactorily up to 1874. In that year there was a famine in Bengal, and the Government had to buy rice in Burma and send it to Bengal for relief purposes. The rice had to be paid for in cash; but when the Government intimated to the Bank of Bombay that they would have to draw out about 30 lakhs (£300,000), their balance at the Bank then being about a crore (£1,000,000), the Bank was unable to let them have the money. In the correspondence which the Viceroy (Lord Northbrook) raised in regard to this, the Secretary of State

(Lord Salisbury) suggested that the Government should release themselves from their engagement to leave their whole balances with the Banks and that they should retain the surplus in their own Treasury, or "lend it for short terms under suitable conditions as to interest and security." This interesting suggestion, closely anticipating more recent proposals, was not acted on, the Indian authorities thinking it improper that the Government should appear to enter into competition with the Banks. But in 1876 the Reserve Treasury system was set up, the Government undertaking to leave, ordinarily, certain minimum amounts at the Banks and diverting the bulk of the rest of their funds into their own Reserve Treasury. In 1878 it proved inconvenient to divert from the Banks immediately the whole of the proceeds of a newly raised loan, and the Comptroller-General was told that he "would be at liberty, to the extent to which he could conveniently do so, to accommodate the Banks with temporary advances from the Reserve Treasury, provided they were willing to pay interest on such advances at the current rates." No special security was taken from the Banks for the sums thus lent to them. For some time loans were freely given in this way. In 1889 the Government declared "that any assistance in relief of the Money Market which may be afforded by means of the Treasury Reserve can only be made (1) through the Bank, (2) at its published rate of discount, (3) in relief of temporary stringency." Up to 1892, however, loans were made as before. From 1892 to 1899 loans were made very rarely. In 1899 the Secretary of State wrote to the authorities in India:—"I see no objection to your lending to the Presidency Banks, on the security of Government paper, at such rates of interest from time to time and for such periods as you think best. I am inclined to think that the rate should, as a rule, be not below the Bank rate." Between 1899 and 1906 such loans were made on four or five occasions; but since 1906 there have been none. The balances left with the Banks without interest normally exceed, however, the prescribed minima.[1]

The question of the proper employment of the Indian Cash Balances is, therefore, a very old one, and one in regard to which the Government have pursued no consistent policy. The effect of recent practice, however, has been on the whole to divert more funds than formerly from banking purposes. On the one hand the Government have been less willing to allow the Banks loans in addition to the normal balances kept with them, and on the other hand the general level of the cash balances has been getting higher.

While the Government's practice has become

[1] All this refers to the balances at the Head Offices. "There is no limit to the Government deposits at branch offices. But the latter are held absolutely at call, and in actual practice are removed with the utmost freedom."—Brunyate, *loc. cit.* p. 98.

stricter, it is arguable, I think, that there is less need for it. Originally, we have seen, the Government banked with the Presidency Banks, and difficulties arose because, the Government's deposits bearing a high proportion to the Bank's total resources, it was not easy to release a large part of these deposits suddenly. This would no longer be the case to nearly the same extent, even if the Government were to place much larger sums with the Banks. In 1870[1] the public deposits at £3,600,000 fell not far short of the total private deposits and exceeded by 50 per cent the capital and reserve of the Banks; in 1880 they were £1,900,000, and were about one-third of the private deposits; in 1890 the figures were £2,400,000, equal to about a quarter of the private deposits; in 1900, £1,900,000, equal to less than a quarter; in 1912 the Government deposits at £2,500,000 were not much more than a tenth of the private deposits. Moreover, the capital and reserves of the Banks have doubled since 1870.

37. The portion of the Cash Balances deposited, under the above arrangements, with the three Presidency Banks varies, of course, from week to week. The amount normally placed with the Head Offices of the Banks has fluctuated for some time in the neighbourhood of £1,000,000. In addition to this, further sums, fluctuating about £1,500,000, are held at branch offices of the Banks. These are deposited

[1] See table given on p. 204.

on a different understanding (see p. 184, footnote) from that governing the sums at the Head Offices, and are held literally at call, the amounts at particular branches being subject to wide variations. The total sums placed with the Banks, head and branch offices together, are usually about £2,000,000, and the maximum deposits in recent years have been about £3,000,000. On these deposits, as in the case of the Bank of England and the British Government deposits, the Banks pay no interest. The whole of the rest of the Government Balances is maintained in cash (rupees, notes, or sovereigns) in the various Government Treasuries. This is the present position. The Government are free in exceptional circumstances, as we have seen above, to place additional sums with the Presidency Banks on which interest is payable. But advantage has not been taken of these powers recently.

38. In view of the facts mentioned at the end of § 36, I am of opinion that the Reserve Treasury system needs reconsideration and that at present rather more funds, perhaps, than is necessary are withdrawn from the use of the Money Market into the Treasuries.

But the critics referred to in § 35 are following a false track when they argue that much offence lies in the present use of the Cash Balances, and that the main remedy for the seasonal stringency of the Indian Money Market is to be found in lending out these balances in India during the busy season. In thinking that any substantial remedy is to be obtained by loans from this source, they are paying too much attention to the transient circumstances of a single year. I believe, for the reasons given below, that the Indian Money Market cannot expect very much assistance from the Cash Balances, and that they have much more to hope for in the future from the growing resources of the Paper Currency Reserve.

Only under one or other of two conditions could loans from the Cash Balances be important: first, if the proceeds of taxation tended to accumulate in the Government Treasuries in the autumn and winter months so that the balances tended to be above their normal level at the busy season; and second, if the Government were to pursue the foolish policy of habitually keeping more ample balances than they really required. The first of these conditions is not fulfilled to any important extent. The land tax is collected, naturally, *after* the harvest has been sold, not during it; and at the end of the calendar year the surplus balances are small. The totals of the Indian Balances on August 1 and January 1 of recent years are shown below:—

(In Lakhs of Rupees)

	August 1.		January 1.	
	Reserve Treasuries.	Total Balances in India.	Reserve Treasuries.	Total Balances in India.
1906–1907	5,26	17,18	1,60	10,46
1907–1908	5,18	17,14	3,20	11,84
1908–1909	7,41	19,54	76	9,33
1909–1910	2,22	13,61	1,74	10,16
1910–1911	9,49	21,43	2,82	13,18
1911–1912	9,62	22,66	3,21	15,18
1912–1913	10,96	24,58	10,62	21,99

The total balances include the working balances in the innumerable District Treasuries all over India and the sums already deposited with the Presidency Banks. When, therefore, we are considering to what extent the Government could lend at the height of the busy season, we must chiefly pay attention to the sums in the *Reserve* Treasuries on Jauuary 1. The above figures show conclusively that, as a rule, the Indian Money Market cannot expect substantial assistance from this source at the time of year when it is most needed. Except in 1913,[1] the resources of the Reserve Treasuries on January 1 have been in recent years between £1,000,000 and £2,000,000.

After January 1, it is true, the revenue comes in rapidly.[2] But, as a matter of fact, the funds which

[1] The exceptional circumstances of 1913 are dealt with in Chap. VIII.

[2] See Report of Comptroller of Currency, 1911–12: "In July the balance generally reaches its highest level. From July onwards until December the revenue collections are comparatively small and the balances steadily go down till they reach their minimum level in November or December. After December the surplus revenue receipts far exceed the demands for expenditure."

accumulate from the proceeds of revenue between January and April are quickly released and returned to the Money Market, as matters now are, through the encashment of the Council Bills which are generally sold in large quantities at this time of year. If this money were to be released by loan instead of by the encashment of Council Bills, the effect would be that less funds would be remitted to London; and unless we assume that more funds are being remitted to London than are really required, this would put the Secretary of State to inconvenience in meeting the Home Charges. Only in years when sufficient funds had been remitted to London earlier in the financial year, therefore, would surplus funds be available in the Indian Treasury to any important extent even in the latter half of the busy season.

I do not say that the Government should not lend from the Cash Balances in India whenever exceptional circumstances may lead to their being at an unnecessarily high level in the busy season. But the sums which could be lent in this way would not generally be important, and the amount of elasticity which the financial system could gain by these loans would be small compared with what it might acquire from a reform of the Paper Currency Reserve. I should prefer, therefore, that the Indian Cash Balances should be held, so far as possible, in notes, thus increasing the capacity of the Currency Reserve, and that all advances should be made in form from the

Currency Reserve. The question of the use of funds in the Cash Balances would then lapse into the question of the use of funds in the Paper Currency Reserve. But if a different system of book-keeping be preferred, no substantial change is involved in what I propose. The method of loaning from the Currency Reserve is applicable *mutatis mutandis* to loans from the Cash Balances.

39. Of the Cash Balances in London no more than a working account is kept with the Bank of England. The manner in which the rest is dealt with is best described in the words of an official memorandum issued by the India Office in 1913 [Cd. 6619]:—

> The practice followed since 1838 has been to keep a certain part of the balance at the Bank (of England) and to lend the remainder at interest. The usual method is to lend to certain banks, discount houses, and stock-brokers of high standing, whose names are included in an approved list, now containing sixty-two names. The list is revised periodically, and applications for admission are carefully considered with reference to the standing and resources of the applicants and the nature of their business. Loans to borrowers on the approved list are granted as a rule for periods from three to five weeks, occasionally for six weeks, so that the whole balance could, if needed, be called in within six weeks. The Accountant-General informs the Secretary of State's broker daily of the amount of loans that may be renewed, the amount of new loans that may be placed, or the amount that must be called. The broker is responsible for obtaining the best possible rate of interest. The amount of a loan is not paid out from the Secretary of State's account at the Bank of England until the security has been lodged

at the Bank. In 1909 it was found that the borrowers on the approved list could not take the full amount of the balances available for loan; and, in order to obtain employment for the funds, the broker was instructed, as a temporary measure, to deposit the excess amount from time to time with leading London banks, usually for periods of between one and three months.

40. In the autumn of 1912 a determined attack was made, in the Press and by means of questions in the House of Commons, on the management of the English Balances, as described above, and on their amount. Many of the questions were framed rather with some other object than to elicit information. But they undoubtedly had the result that the authorities published to the public much ampler details than were previously available. A valuable summary of these will be found in the official memorandum [Cd. 6619] from which I have just quoted.[1] As the outcome of this very full inquisition into the whole subject, only two points have emerged in which, in my opinion, the authorities are open to criticism in detail—*i.e.* apart from wide questions of policy. They renewed India Bills (which were eventually paid off in December 1912) when they could have very well afforded to discharge them. If the season of 1912–13 had been a bad one, or if their expectations had been upset in any other way, it would always have been open to the India Council to issue the Bills afresh. Their action appears to the

[1] See also Lord Inchcape's letter to the *Times* of November 12, 1912. I forbear to enter in detail into what is not, in reality, one of the truly vital aspects of Indian Government Finance.

outside critic to have been one of ill-considered caution. The other point is a trifle and reflects, perhaps, on a curiosity of our economic organism rather than on the India Office. It was slightly shocking to discover that the Government broker, who is not even a whole-time officer, and has a separate business of his own besides his official duties, is the highest paid[1] official of the Government with the sole exception of the Viceroy. He has probably been paid too high even on current city standards. But it suggests once again the old question how long it will be found necessary to pay city men so entirely out of proportion to what other servants of society commonly receive for performing social services not less useful or difficult.

41. Some of the conclusions of this chapter may be summarised. All countries, since the practice has been generally adopted of employing a medium of exchange composed of some cheaper material than the standard of value, must keep a monetary reserve. Where there is a State bank, the bank is usually entrusted with this duty. Where the State regulates the currency and the note issue without the intervention of a bank the State must itself undertake it.

[1] The payments to the Government broker, from which, no doubt, some deduction has to be made for expenses, have been as follows :—

1908	£2,642	1911	£10,544
1909	6,396	1912 (up to Dec. 14) .	7,958
1910	12,728		

The principles governing the amount of these payments were explained in the House of Commons on December 17, 1912, in answer to a question.

The proper magnitude of the reserve must depend upon the particular circumstances of each country. In India the reserve must be unusually large, first, because India is a great country specially liable to wide fluctuations in her prosperity and trade on account of climatic conditions the character of which cannot be easily foreseen; and second, because a large amount of foreign capital is employed, not only in permanent investment, but in temporary loans withdrawable at short notice, and because against these foreign liabilities India holds no appreciable amount of international Stock Exchange securities capable of easy realisation. I have argued that £40,000,000 may be, perhaps, at present a suitable amount to be held by Government in its sterling Reserves. These Reserves are most useful if they are held in London, where they must necessarily be wanted whenever there is need to make use of them. In deference to a public opinion which does not clearly understand the purpose of the Reserves or the limitations under which the Secretary of State must needs act in managing his sterling resources, it may be worth while to allay a groundless suspicion by the compromise of holding a fair proportion of the reserve of actual gold coin in India herself. When a Reserve of some such amount as the above has been firmly established, the diversion of further funds into any form of sterling or into the London Market should be deliberately avoided.

Stability has been attained already, or is about to

be. So, on the whole, has economy, though some current opinion in regard to the use of gold puts it in jeopardy. The system still wants elasticity. A machinery ought to be set up, therefore, by which further funds, accumulating in the hands of Government through the increased use of notes, may be used in India to afford the needed elasticity in the seasonal supply of currency.

Let the Indian public learn that it is extravagant to use gold as a medium of exchange, foolish to lessen the utility of their reserves through suspicion of the London Money Market, and highly advantageous to their own trade and to the resources of their own money market to develop the use of notes; and their financial system may soon become wonderfully well adapted to the particular circumstances of their situation. The history of the last twelve years has been transitional. The authorities have been—wisely—building up the reserves they ought to have. This process has necessarily diverted funds from the Indian Money Market, and has naturally excited some measure of opposition. But the fruits of cautious growth may soon be reaped.

CHAPTER VII

INDIAN BANKING

1. In passing from Currency and the Finance of Government to the kindred topic of Banking, we come to a part of the subject where statistics and other information are much less freely available to the outside critic. The published figures are not adequate to tell us much of what we require to know, and the literature of Indian Banking is almost non-existent. I must run the risk, therefore, of sometimes falling into errors of fact, and hope that, if these errors provoke criticism, they will bring to light the true facts at the same time.

2. The Money Market and Banking System of India comprises the following as its four main constituents :—

(i.) The Presidency Banks; (ii.) the European Exchange Banks ; (iii.) the Indian Joint Stock Banks ; and (iv.) the Shroffs, Marwaris, and other private bankers and money-lenders.

The first two of these constitute what we may term the European Money Market, and the rest, under the leadership of Marwaris and Parsees, the Indian or Native Money Market,—up-country Banks such as the Allahabad Bank and the Alliance Bank of Simla, which are Indian Joint Stock Banks under European management, occupying, perhaps, an intermediate position. The local money markets, outside the main towns in which European business men have offices and where the bulk of the foreign trade is handled, are entirely in the hands of Indians.

3. How close a connexion exists between the two money markets—native and European—how nearly the rates ruling in one agree with those in the other, and how readily capital flows from one to the other, I am not clear. Some evidence bearing on these points was laid before the Fowler Committee of 1898, but such facts are now fifteen years old. In the pre-1899 period it was not uncommon in times of stringency for the bazaar rate to be appreciably lower than the Presidency Bank rate, and the connexion between the two money markets seems to have been very incomplete. The following quotation from a letter by Mr. J. H. Sleigh, Secretary and Treasurer of the Bank of Bombay, written in 1898 (reprinted in the Appendix to the Fowler Committee's Report), is interesting :—

> During the last export season, Shroffs' 60 days' sight bills were not obtainable over 8 per cent discount. . . . This was the rate then ruling in the native bazaar both in Bombay and Calcutta, and that, too, while the Exchange

Banks were greedy to receive fixed deposits for short periods at 9, 10, and even 11 per cent per annum, and while the Presidency Banks were straining to meet the demands for loans at 12 and 13 per cent per annum. But there is no singularity in these facts. The same peculiarity has shown itself over and over again during periods of financial pressure; and even at the present moment (November 1898), while money is not by any means tight, there exists a difference of about 2 per cent between the bazaar and the Presidency Bank rates. I have ever found that when the official rate rose abnormally high, the rate in the native market did not respond to the full extent, but generally stopped at 7 or 8 per cent, though the Presidency Banks' rate might rise to 10 or 12 per cent. The explanation is simple. The Shroffs, who finance nearly the whole of the internal trade of India, rarely, if ever, discount European Paper and never purchase foreign or sterling bills. Neither do they lend money on Government Paper or similar securities, but confine their advances to the discount of *hoondees*, to loans to cultivators, and against gold and silver bullion. The *hoondees* they purchase are for the most part those of traders, small and large, at rates of discount ranging from 9 to 25 per cent per annum, but the *hoondees* they buy and sell to each other, which are chiefly the traders' *hoondees* bearing the Shroffs' own endorsements, rule the rates in the native bazaar, and are generally negotiated, during the busy season, at from 5 to 8 per cent discount. They also discount their endorsements pretty largely with the Presidency Banks when rates are low, and discontinue doing so when they rise above 6 per cent. They also speculate largely at times in Government Paper, especially during the off season, but rarely or ever hold it or lend on it.

I have seen no evidence for supposing that the general conditions outlined in this quotation do not still hold; but in recent years the Presidency Bank rates have not risen above 9 per cent, and occasions for the operation of the tendencies described above have been rarer. The conditions prevailing in the Indian Money Market in the period immediately preceding 1898 were in many respects very abnormal. I suspect that the rates in the two markets may appear to be more different than they really are, and are explicable by the difference of the conditions and of security, subject to which business is transacted. It is, however, plain that the main movements of the interest rate up and down, which result from the central facts of the Indian seasons and harvests, must be the same in both markets, and that the Native Money Market must ultimately depend on the European for additional supplies of cash.

4. As I am chiefly interested in the Indian Banking System, so far as this book is concerned, from the point of view of its effect on the remittance of funds to and from India, I shall be concerned for the most part with what I have called the European Money Market—the Presidency and Exchange Banks. But an Indian writer, in a position to know the facts, could throw much useful light on a question where I must necessarily be content with somewhat doubtful conjecture.

5. The Presidency Bank of Bengal was opened in 1806 and received its charter of incorporation from

the East India Company in 1809.[1] The first Bank of Bombay[2] was established under a similar charter in 1840, and the Bank of Madras in 1843. The establishment of these Banks in the other Presidencies put an end to the possibility that the Bank of Bengal might become a Bank for all India. The Presidency Banks had, at first, a semi-official character. At the foundation of the Bank of Bengal, the East India Company contributed one-fifth (the proportion became smaller subsequently) of the capital and appointed three of the directors. Up to the time of the Mutiny the office of Secretary and Treasurer was held by a Covenanted Civilian.

Up to 1862 the Banks had the right of note issue; but this right was so hedged about by a restriction of the total liabilities payable on demand to a certain multiple (at first three times, later four times) of the cash reserve, and of the total liabilities of all kinds to the amount of the Bank's capital (up to 1839), or of the total note issue to a fixed amount (from 1839 to 1862), that the note issue of the Presidency Banks never became important. In 1862 the management of the note issue was taken over by the Government in the manner described in Chapter III. At the same time the right of note issue by private

[1] See Mr. J. B. Brunyate's *Account of the Presidency Banks* (1900), whence the historical details which follow have been chiefly derived. Mr. Brunyate's *Account* is of the highest value to students of banking history.

[2] The first Bank of Bombay went into liquidation in 1868, although its liabilities were eventually paid up in full. A new Bank of Bombay was formed in the same year.

Banks was finally abolished.[1] In 1876 the Government relinquished their share of the capital of the Banks and their right of appointing directors.[2] Since then the Presidency Banks have lost their official character, but remain distinct from other Banks in that they are governed by a special Charter Act (the Presidency Banks Act of 1876).

6. The Presidency Banks have worked from the beginning under very rigorous restrictions as to the character of the business which they might undertake. These restrictions were originally due partly, perhaps, to a feeling of jealousy on the part of the Court of Directors of the East India Company lest the Banks should compete in business (such as foreign exchange) which the Company regarded as its own; but chiefly from a proper wish that semi-official institutions, in a country so dangerous for banking as India, should

[1] By 1862 such issues were of negligible account, but in earlier times they had been important. "Probably the first banking institution in India, on European lines, was the Bank of Hindustan, which was established in Calcutta about 1770 by a private trading firm. The notes of this Bank, though not recognised by the Government, obtained a local circulation which occasionally reached forty or fifty lakhs and generally averaged about half that amount.' It is said that they were "received for many years at all the public offices in Calcutta scarcely excepting the Treasury itself." On two occasions, once in 1819 and again in 1829, the occurrence of a panic led to the presentation for payment of about twenty lakhs' worth of the notes, and the demand was promptly met. (Brunyate, *loc. cit.* p. 55.) This Bank and others disappeared in the commercial disasters of 1829-1832. "Out of their ruin rose the Union Bank, a Joint Stock Bank created by co-operation among all the leading Calcutta houses." (Brunyate, *loc. cit.* p. 59.) In 1834 the Bank of Bengal refused to accept the notes of its formidable rival, and in 1848 the Union Bank disappeared.

[2] This was in some degree consequent on the failure of the Bank of Bombay in 1868, the Government having found itself in the awkward position of being a shareholder in a Bank, its liability for which was not clearly defined.

be conducted on the safest possible principles.[1] An exceedingly interesting history of the restrictions is to be found in Mr. Brunyate's *Account.* In 1862 they were greatly relaxed, but the most important limitations were reimposed in 1876.[2] Since that time only minor charges have been effected.

7. The principal restrictions on the Presidency Banks are now the following:—

(i.) The Banks may not draw, discount, buy, or sell bills of exchange or other negotiable securities *unless they are payable in India*[3] or in Ceylon; this restriction has cut off the Presidency Banks completely from dealing in sterling drafts or any kind of foreign exchange; (ii.) they may not borrow, or receive deposits payable, outside India, or maintain a foreign branch or agency for this or similar purposes, and they are thus prevented from raising funds in London for use in India[4]; (iii.) they may not lend

[1] The way in which Indian institutions have been moulded on and influenced by English is interestingly illustrated by the fact that several of the provisions in the Charters of the Presidency Banks were copied from the 1695 constitution of the Bank of England.

[2] This also was partly consequent on the failure of the Bank of Bombay in 1868.

[3] Except for the use of principals for the purpose of certain specified kinds of remittance.

[4] In 1877 the Banks pressed strongly for a relaxation of this provision. But the Secretary of State held that "the concession of a power of creating a foreign agency in England, such as would be the result of entering into loan transactions of the nature of those contemplated, would admit of the Banks locking up a large portion of their capital at so great a distance as to render it practically unavailable in the case of any emergency arising in India." This argument is not one which would be likely to be used at the present time. The fear would rather be lest they should lock up funds in India.

for a longer period than six months[1]; (iv.) or upon mortgage, or in any other manner upon the security of immovable property; (v.) or upon promissory notes bearing less than two independent names; (vi.) or upon personal security; (vii.) or upon goods, unless the goods, or the title to them, are deposited with the Bank as security.

The fifth of these provisions allows a loophole by means of which the rules can be made to work in practice less rigorously than appears on paper. Any two names will satisfy the letter of the Presidency Banks Act; but any two names are not necessarily very good security. After getting two names to satisfy the Act, the authorities of the Banks can then proceed to satisfy the dictates of cautious banking by taking, as well, some of the other kinds of security upon which, technically, they are forbidden to lend. It is an excellent instance of the consequences of an attempt to control banking by an elaborate Act forty years old. The last provision has led, I believe, to the Banks establishing a kind of bonded warehouse for the reception of merchandise. In other cases the borrower's own mill or warehouse is made to serve the purpose by the expedient of the Bank's paying the wages of his watchman. Where the personal security of the borrower is obviously good, there must be a temptation to allow him to value the goods generously, rather than to put the Bank to the in-

[1] Up to 1907 the maximum period was three months.

convenience of housing or watching a greater bulk of merchandise.

As some recompense for these restrictions, the Presidency Banks have been allowed to hold a portion of the Government balances without payment of interest. The use of these balances was first granted them in 1862 as compensation for their being deprived of the right of note issue. Up to 1876 the Presidency Banks held, subject to certain conditions, the *whole* of the Government balances which would have been "paid in ordinary course into Government Treasuries at the places where the head offices and branch offices of the Banks are established." But on more than one occasion the Banks made difficulties when the Government desired to withdraw large sums at short notice. In 1876, therefore, the Reserve Treasuries were established, and since that time only a portion of the balances has been placed with the Banks.[1]

8. The present constitution of the Presidency Banks is to be explained, therefore, by their long and complicated history. The restrictions under which they work have in the past contributed, beyond doubt, to their stability. The Bank of Bengal has seen the rise and fall of numerous powerful rivals. Only by virtue of its being absolutely precluded by law from the more speculative forms of business, has this Bank survived the half-dozen or more violent crises by which the Indian

[1] See §§ 36-38 of Chapter VI.

financial system has been assailed in the last hundred years. And, in spite of the restrictions, the Presidency Banks have shown great vitality and a power of expansion hardly less than that of the Exchange Banks in the happier circumstances of the last decade. But their constitutions are exceedingly out of date at the present time. The considerations which originally gave rise to them are no longer operative;—since the introduction of the Gold Standard, for example, dealing in foreign exchange has ceased to be a highly speculative business. And they do not play as useful a part in the Indian Financial System as with a different history behind them they might do.

9. The principal statistics of the three Presidency Banks are as follows[1]:—

Dec. 31.	Capital, Reserve, and Rest.	Public Deposits.	Private Deposits.	Cash.
1870	£2,412,000	£3,620,000	£4,264,000	£6,646,000
1880	2,702,000	1,941,000	5,662,000	4,943,000
1890	2,984,000	2,395,000	9,842,000[1]	8,645,000[1]
1895	3,267,000	2,218,000	8,747,000	5,131,000
1900	3,731,000	1,870,000	8,588,000	3,363,000
1905	4,156,000	2,078,000	14,842,000	5,487,000
1906	4,266,000	2,052,000	18,301,000	7,300,000
1907	4,366,000	2,239,000	18,742,000	6,350,000
1908	4,461,000	2,172,000	19,077,000	6,925,000
1909	4,521,000	2,132,000	21,767,000	7,770,000
1910	4,607,000	2,824,000	21,563,000	7,567,000
1911[2]	4,650,000	2,640,000	23,250,000	9,430,000
1912[2]	4,900,000	2,530,000	24,000,000	8,070,000

1 An exceptional year, due to the excessive abundance of money.

2 The figures for 1911 and 1912 are not taken from the same returns as the rest, and are not quite strictly comparable with them in one or two details.

The rupee has been converted at the uniform rate of 1s. 4d. throughout.

These figures do not require much comment. The growth of private deposits since 1900 (rising from £8,500,000 in 1900 to £15,000,000 in 1905 and £24,000,000 in 1912) is very noticeable. This has been accompanied by a fair increase of Capital and Reserve and of Cash. The Presidency Banks publish weekly statements of their affairs, and it is scarcely possible, therefore, that they should "window-dress" their balance sheets. The figures given above refer to December 31, which falls in the busy season; and the proportion of cash held affords no ground of complaint. It should be said, however, that, while the public deposits at the head offices are stable and not liable to sudden reduction, the public deposits at the branch offices stand in a different position and are held literally at call. It is necessary for the Banks to hold a considerable proportion of these in cash at the branches in question, and this arrangement makes the cash held against the private deposits appear in a somewhat more favourable light than it should. It must also be remembered that the Presidency Banks are to a certain extent Bankers' Banks, and that the other Indian Banks reckon their balances with the Presidency Banks (included in the private deposits) as part of their cash.

10. The two provisions of the Presidency Banks Act which have proved fundamental in their effect on the development of the Indian Banking System are those which prohibit the Presidency Banks from

dealing in foreign exchange and from raising funds in London. To transact these two classes of business —though once established they have not limited their transactions to them—a class of Banks has arisen known as the Exchange Banks. Officially a Bank is an Exchange Bank if its head office is located elsewhere than in India; but Banks in this category coincide very nearly with Banks doing the class of business described above. The Indian Specie Bank is the only Indian Joint Stock Bank having a branch office in London; but this is probably in connexion with its business in silver and pearls, and this Bank does not transact any considerable volume of business of the kind undertaken by Exchange Banks.

11. The Exchange Banks proper fall into two groups—those doing a considerable proportion of their total business in India, and those which are no more than agencies of large banking corporations doing business all over Asia. This second group includes the Comptoir National d'Escompte de Paris, the Yokohama Specie Bank, the Deutsch-Asiatische Bank, the International Banking Corporation, and the Russo-Asiatic Bank. These Banks represent in India, French, Japanese, German, American, and Russian interests respectively. No figures are published of the proportion of their total business which these Banks transact in India. But I should be surprised if, even in the case of the Yokohama Specie Bank, it would amount to more than five to

ten per cent; and in the case of some of them it must be much less than this. In what follows, therefore, I shall leave these five Banks out of account.

In the first group there are six Banks—the Delhi and London Bank (1844), the Chartered Bank of India, Australia, and China (1853), the National Bank of India (1863), the Hong Kong and Shanghai Banking Corporation (1864), the Mercantile Bank of India (1893 [1]), and the Eastern Bank (1910). The dates after these Banks give the years when they were established. Of these, two, the Chartered and the Hong Kong Banks, do a very large business in other parts of the East, especially China [2]; but this does not prevent their Indian connexion from being important. The other four are primarily Indian.[3] It is noticeable that no entirely new Exchange Bank now surviving [4] was founded between 1864 and 1910. This is in spite of the fact that most of the above, especially in the last decade, have proved enormously successful from the point of view of their shareholders. The Delhi and London Bank,[5]

1 This is the date of the foundation of this Bank under its present style, but it was formed out of the old Chartered Mercantile Bank of India, London and China, which dates much further back.

2 The Chartered Bank, in spite of its name, has never done business in Australia.

3 But not exclusively. The National Bank, for example, has a large interest in East Africa; this coast has considerable trade connexions with India, and the rupee has a fairly wide circulation there (see figures of rupees exported given on p. 154).

4 The New Oriental Bank, established in 1885 (the great Oriental Bank Corporation had failed in 1884), went into liquidation in 1893.

5 I fancy that it has more the character of an Indian Joint Stock Bank and less of the character of an Exchange Bank than the others.

the oldest established of all, has not shown the vitality or power of expansion of the others; and the Eastern Bank, though it seems to have made a good start, is still too young to pass judgment on. But the shares of the rest, if the issue of bonus shares be allowed for, stand at a premium of about 200 per cent or more. It is probable, however, that it would be exceedingly difficult to start a new Exchange Bank at the present time, except under the aegis of some important financial house already established in a strong position in India.[1] Indian Exchange Banking is no business for speculative or enterprising outsiders, and the large profits which it earns are protected by established and not easily assailable advantages.

12. This summary leads us, therefore, to the important conclusion that the business of financing Indian trade, so far as it is carried out by Banks with their seat in London,[2] is in the hands of a very small number of Banks. They stand, broadly speaking, in an exceedingly strong financial position supported by large reserve funds. In this matter India is now enjoying the fruit of past disasters and of conditions in which the struggle for existence was too keen to

[1] The Eastern Bank was established under the auspices of Messrs. E. D. Sassoon, while two important French Banks and Messrs. Brown, Shipley, and Co. are represented on the board of directors.

[2] There is of course much business of a semi-banking character transacted by financial and mercantile houses, some of them of the first magnitude, with establishments both in India and London. But they are private firms and publish no information about their business of which it is possible to take account.

allow any but the fittest to survive. If the present spell of prosperity lasts too long, she will no doubt lose it.

13. I shall not attempt any complete account of the activities of a typical Exchange Bank. Much of their business is very like that of any other Bank. But it will be worth while to describe in rather more detail the most characteristic part of their transactions and the part which is most relevant to the topics of this book.

14. In addition to its capital and the reserves accumulated from profits, an Exchange Bank obtains its funds by receiving deposits either for fixed periods or on current account. These deposits are received both in India and in London; but it is a principal object of Exchange Banks to obtain as much as they can in London, and they seek to attract such deposits by offering better terms than an English Bank will allow. On fixed deposits, received for a year or more, 4 or $3\frac{1}{2}$ per cent will be paid; for shorter periods a more variable rate; and on current accounts 2 per cent will be allowed on the minimum monthly balance or on the amount by which the balance exceeds a certain fixed minimum. Apart from the cash, money at call, and investments, which every Bank must hold, a certain part of these funds are employed in making loans either in India or elsewhere. But a large part is employed in the purchase (or discount)

of bills of exchange. Some of these bills will be negotiated in London and drawn on India, but the bulk of them will be negotiated in India and drawn on London. A busy Exchange Bank discounts far more of these trade bills in India than it can afford to hold until maturity. But as they are drawn on London houses there is no difficulty in rediscounting them in London. As the majority of the bills are bought by the Banks *in India*, while cash is received for them, either at maturity or through rediscount, *in London*, the Banks are constantly in the position of finding themselves in funds in London and of wishing to have funds (for the purchase of more bills) in India. They proceed, therefore, to even up their accounts as between London and India by buying, in London, Council Bills (or transfers) or sovereigns (from the Bank of England or from the agents of Egyptian or Australian Banks) for delivery in India, or, perhaps, silver (though their dealings in silver bullion are probably much less important than formerly)[1] for remittance to India. The question of what determines the relative advantages of these methods has been discussed in Chapter V.

The demand for Council Bills, therefore, chiefly depends on how much new business the Exchange Banks are entering into in India. The method of telegraphic transfers enables them to act with great

[1] Another method occasionally worth while employing is the purchase of Government Rupee Paper in London and its sale in India.

despatch on receiving advices from their Indian agents. The Indian branches obtain immediately the funds enabling them to take the trade bills, the offer of which had seemed to them to be at sufficiently satisfactory rates to make the transaction taken as a whole worth while. A few weeks later the bills reach England, are duly accepted, and are capable of being rediscounted if the Bank needs additional free funds to buy more Council Bills and turn its money over again in another transaction of the same kind.

We are now in a position to understand what the Secretary of State means when he says that he has sold bills to meet the needs of trade. If he withdraws the convenience of telegraphic transfers or forces the Banks to put themselves in funds in India by sending sovereigns, he causes delay or additional expense in the discounting of bills in India. In other words, Indian traders are less easily able to turn the goods they are exporting into money. On the other hand, if the Indian season is a poor one and the exports fall off, the offer of bills for discount is reduced and the need of the Exchange Banks in London to buy Council Bills correspondingly less.

It is worth noticing that, from the point of view of the London Money Market as a whole, it is a mere difference of machinery whether the Exchange Banks finance the Indian trade by attracting deposits in London and hold the bills themselves, or whether the Discount Houses and London Banks attract the deposits and use them to rediscount bills for the Exchange Banks. In so far as the Exchange Banks can attract deposits themselves without paying too high a rate for them, this alternative is usually the more profitable for them,—especially since, if they are able to hold in this way a considerable proportion of the bills they discount, they can afford to wait for a favourable moment before rediscounting such bills as they have eventually to dispose of. But, apart from private profits, the important point is the extent to which Indian trade is financed by the purchase of Council Bills in London with borrowed money, whether this money is supplied by the depositors in Exchange Banks or by those who rediscount the bills.

15. There is, *prima facie*, some danger to the stability of the Indian financial system in the fact that its money market is largely financed by funds raised, not permanently but for short periods, in a far-distant foreign centre.[1] In order to judge accurately whether this danger is in any way a real one, it would be necessary to have before us certain facts which are not ordinarily published. We do not know what proportion of the Exchange Banks' total deposits are held in England; or to what extent those which

[1] The volume of bills, drawn in India on London and outstanding, is not, of course, a correct measure of the extent to which India is being financed abroad. A bill may be used to finance the foreign purchaser just as much as the Indian seller. For example, a dealer in cotton in India might be paid by a 3 m/s Bank credit supplied by the buyer, a Continental spinner; this spinner might get the cotton within a fortnight of the acceptance of the bill, which would, therefore, be really financing his cotton factory.

are so held are fixed for a year or more and how far they are at call or short notice. As is often the case when banking is under discussion in other countries, those who are in a position to know are not in a position to speak, while those who are in a position to speak are not in a position to know. I will make my guess for what it is worth in § 18. In the meantime let us discuss the principle which should guide us, had we knowledge.

It is plain that if Banks were to borrow money at short notice in England and use it in India—certainly if they were to do this on a large scale,—the situation might be dangerous. They might be called on to return what they had borrowed in England, and unable at short notice to bring back what they had lent in India. The principle of which we are in search is, therefore, that the sums borrowed on relatively short notice in either country should not exceed the assets located there. Where, however, bills of exchange between England and India are in question, it is not immediately plain what part of the Banks' funds may properly be regarded as located in England and what part in India. The answer is, I think, that a bill which has been accepted in England, and is payable there at maturity, is an English asset, wherever it may have been originally negotiated. Thus in the case of Indian Exchange Banks, their deposits in London (other than those fixed for long periods) should be at least balanced by their short-term loans in London, their cash in London, their portfolio of trade bills having a London domicile, and such of their securities as may be readily marketable in London. Similarly their liquid assets in India should at least balance their short-period liabilities there.

16. How far these conditions are as a matter of fact satisfied, it is, as I have said above, impossible to know for certain. The Exchange Banks do not distinguish in their published accounts between their Indian and London deposits. They do, however, give private information to the Indian authorities of their deposits in India and elsewhere respectively in each year. These aggregates for all the Exchange Banks together are published in the *Statistics of British India*, Part II., and are, therefore, available to the public two or three years after the period to which they refer.[1]

So far as the Indian deposits are concerned, these returns are very valuable. But the aggregate of deposits outside India is as nearly as possible useless. For Exchange Banks of both groups—the Banks primarily Indian and the agencies of huge European institutions doing business in many parts of the world—are lumped together, so that the total includes the whole of the French deposits of the Comptoir National d'Escompte and of the deposits, in whatever country, of the other Banks with Indian agencies enumerated

[1] The figures for 1910, for example, are in the issue which was obtainable in England early in 1913.

on p. 206. The figures are, therefore, hardly relevant to questions peculiarly Indian; and I will content myself with quoting, from the table given in the official statistics, the total deposits of Exchange Banks made *in India*, and the cash balances held *in India* against them.

EXCHANGE BANKS

	Deposits in India.	Cash Balances in India.
1890	£5,000,000	£2,300,000
1895	6,900,000	1,800,000
1900	7,000,000	1,600,000
1901	7,900,000	2,200,000
1902	9,100,000	2,300,000
1903	10,800,000	2,100,000
1904	10,900,000	3,300,000
1905	11,400,000	2,500,000
1906	12,100,000	3,400,000
1907	12,800,000	3,700,000
1908	13,000,000	2,500,000
1909	13,500,000	2,800,000
1910	16,200,000	2,900,000

17. Two facts emerge from this table with great plainness—the rapid rate at which in recent years Exchange Banks have been able to increase the funds raised by deposit in India herself, and the slow rate at which they have thought fit to increase their Indian balances.[1] The position has evidently changed a good deal in quite recent times. It is tantalising to think that two years must elapse before we can

[1] On the one hand, these balances are even weaker than they look, because they include the Exchange Banks' balances at the Presidency Banks. On the other hand, the Exchange Banks often have sovereigns or Council Bills in transit which they may fairly consider, perhaps, as equivalent to cash.

know how the Banks stood in these respects last December (1912). The *Statistics of British India* do not lend their aid to ruder hands than those of the historian.

In the event of an internal financial crisis in India the Exchange Banks are probably depending on the anticipation that they will be able to remit funds from London by telegraphic transfer. In this case they rely on not being hard pressed in India and in London at the same time. An Indian reserve, such as they appear to keep, of from 18 to 20 per cent would be respectable, for example, in England. But in such a country as India, where banking is ill-established and hoarding more than a memory, the proportion held in reserve seems somewhat lower than perhaps it ought to be. Possibly Exchange Banks have already been in smooth waters longer than is for their good. There are famous dates in the history of Indian banking which should serve as a *memento mori.*

18. When we turn to the assets and liabilities of the Exchange Banks in England we find reason for supposing a much stronger position; for the bulk of the bills of exchange held are probably domiciled in London and may be regarded, therefore, as liquid London assets.[1] The following table sets out the

[1] A certain proportion of their bills, no doubt, are drawn on the London branches of Banks with a foreign domicile. These bills are not always so readily discountable as London acceptances, the Bank of England taking them unwillingly and charging ¼ per cent extra discount. But for the present purpose they can, I think, be regarded none the less as liquid London assets.

figures relating to deposits, leaving out the Hong Kong and Shanghai Banking Corporation, because, although its Indian business is important, this can only be a small proportion of its total business. I include all the other Banks given in my first group (see p. 207) although the non-Indian business of the Chartered and National Banks cannot be accurately allowed for.

FIXED AND CURRENT DEPOSITS (IN £1,000,000)

Bank.	1900.	1905.	1906.	1907.	1908.	1909.	1910.	1911.	1912.
	£m.	£m.	£m.	£m.	£m.	£m.	£m.	£m.	£m.
Chartered . .	9¼	11½	13¼	12¼	12½	13¾	15½	16¼	18
National . .	6	9	9¾	10¼	10¼	11¾	12¾	13	14
Mercantile . .	1½	2¾	3¾	3½	3½	4½	5¼	5½	5½
Delhi and London	1¼	1¼	1¼	1½	1¼	1¼	1½	1½	1½
Eastern . .	...	...	...	...	...	...	1¼	1¾	2
Total . .	18	24½	28	27½	27½	31¼	36¼	38	41

The total cash in hand and at bankers held by these five Banks at the end of 1912 was about £m7¾. I estimate that in 1910 these Banks may have held *outside India* about £m23 in deposits and about £m5 cash in hand and at bankers.

As to the proportion of these deposits which were held for long periods there is no accurate information. The Chartered and Eastern Banks are alone in distinguishing in their balance sheets between fixed deposits and current accounts. In 1912 the Chartered Bank held £m10½ on current account, etc., and £m7½ on fixed deposit; the Eastern Bank £m½ on current account and £m1½ on fixed deposit.[1] More than half of the deposits of the Banks as a whole are probably held on current account or at short notice. If we are to make a guess, the Banks may have held in 1910 about £13,000,000 on current account outside India; but by no means all of this (in the case of the Chartered and National Banks especially) would be held in London. The question of the amount of the London assets of the Banks does not lend itself to statistical summary. But I do not think that there is the least reason for supposing that the position is not a strong one.

19. The principles which underlie the preceding analysis may be illustrated by reference to a hypothetical balance sheet, simplified, but less simplified than those commonly published.

	£m.		£m.
(i.) Capital and Reserve Fund . . .	1½	(vii.) Loans and Advances in London . .	3
(ii.) Fixed Deposits in London . . .	3½	(viii.) Loans and Advances in India . . .	3
(iii.) Current Accounts in London . . .	2½	(ix.) Trade Bills on London negotiated in India .	6½
(iv.) Fixed Deposits in India	2	(x.) Trade Bills on India negotiated in London	1½
(v.) Current Accounts in India . . .	2½	(xi.) Cash, etc., in London	1½
(vi.) Trade Bills on London negotiated in India and rediscounted in London . . .	5½	(xii.) Cash, etc., in India .	½
		(xiii.) Securities . . .	1
		(xiv.) Miscellaneous assets including silver bullion	½
	17½		17½

[1] I believe that the Eastern Bank offers rather better terms than the other Banks for fixed deposits.

This would probably be published as follows:—

	£m.		£m.
Capital and Reserve Fund	$1\frac{1}{2}$	Loans, Advances, etc. .	6
Deposits, etc. . . .	$10\frac{1}{2}$	Bills of Exchange . .	$2\frac{1}{2}$
		Cash, etc.. . . .	2
		Securities . . .	1
		Miscellaneous assets . .	$\frac{1}{2}$
	12		12

[Bills rediscounted and outstanding, £m$5\frac{1}{2}$.]

Acceptances have been omitted in the above, the amount of bills payable is supposed to be deducted from cash, and various minor items are omitted. The "capital employed in India" seems to be (viii.) + (x.) + (xii.) = £m5. The "capital employed in London" is (vii.) + (ix.) − (vi.) + (xi.) = £m$5\frac{1}{2}$.[1] The securities and miscellaneous assets (xiii.) + (xiv.) = £m$1\frac{1}{2}$, may be regarded perhaps as equally available in either centre. If there is a run in India, assets must be available there in a liquid form equal to (v.). If there is a run in London, liquid assets must be available there equal to (iii.). The second condition, but not the first, is, in this hypothetical example, fulfilled. If the Bank had to remit funds back from India to London, this would be most simply effected by not entering into new business under (ix.). It would not then be necessary to buy

[1] The confusing point here is this: that (ix.) is the amount advanced to Indian merchants, and (x.) the amount advanced to English merchants; yet (ix.) must be reckoned an English asset and (x.) an Indian asset. For (ix.) when it falls due is paid in England, although, of course, the Bank has advanced money, through the purchase of it, in India.

Council Bills, and the trade bills already bought under (ix.), being rediscounted or allowed to mature in London, would swell the available funds there automatically. If it were possible to call in loans in India and reduce (viii.), then it would be possible to buy more trade bills under (ix.) in India (or Government sterling drafts if trade were depressed), without having to buy Council Bills in London, and these trade bills could then be rediscounted in London. If the Exchange Banks are remitting funds back to London, this shows itself, therefore, in a poor demand for Council Bills; and conversely when they are remitting funds to India, there is a strong demand for Council Bills. Thus the weakness of the demand for Council Bills in times of depression (and the strength of the demand for Government sterling drafts) partly depends on the action of the Exchange Banks. What their action would be in a situation of acute stringency bordering on financial panic, it is not easy to predict.

20. So far the only apparent element of danger in the banking position seems to lie in the growth of deposits attracted by the Exchange Banks in India without a corresponding growth in their Indian cash reserves. It would be a good thing if the Exchange Banks were compelled to distinguish in their balance sheets between their Indian and extra-Indian business, much in the manner set out in the hypothetical balance sheet on p. 218, except that for "London"

"outside India" would have to be substituted.[1] They should also distinguish, as two already do distinguish, between fixed deposits and accounts at call or for short periods. When, as in the case of the Exchange Banks, we have to deal with a small number of Banks of established position, an insistence on due publicity, rather than compulsion or regulation in matters of policy, is likely to be the proper remedy for any weaknesses which may possibly exist.

21. The next section of the Indian banking world comprises the Indian Joint Stock Banks, *i.e.* those Banks, other than the three Presidency Banks, registered in India and having their head offices there. This is a confusing group, because a great number of small money-lending establishments are registered as Banks under the Indian Companies Act —in 1910–11 492 businesses were classified as Banks.[2] The official statistics separate off, however, those of the Banks proper which are of any considerable size, —those, namely, which have a paid-up capital and reserve of at least 5 lakhs (£33,000).

The earlier Banks, coming under this description, were usually under European management. Out of seven existing in 1870, only two now survive,—the Bank of Upper India (1863) and the Allahabad Bank

[1] It would be most useful to have a triple classification—India, London, and elsewhere. But I do not see how the Indian authorities could reasonably enforce this.

[2] The great majority (363) of these small money-lending establishments were registered in Madras. Most of them are mutual societies, and it would not be difficult to exclude them from the official statistics.

(1865).[1] Between 1870 and 1894 seven more Banks, conforming on the whole to this same type, were founded, of which four now survive,—the Alliance Bank of Simla (1874), the Oudh Commercial Bank (1881), the Punjab Banking Company (1889), and the Punjab National Bank (1894).[2] All these Banks are on a very small scale compared with the Presidency and Exchange Banks; but they are distinguished in type from most of the more recent creations.

Between 1894 and 1904[3] no new Banks were founded with as much as 5 lakhs of paid-up capital. But since 1904 there has been a great outburst of fresh activity, and a type of Bank new to India has become important. The way was led in 1904 by the foundation of the Bank of Burma. This Bank failed in 1911, two directors and the general manager being found guilty of cheating and sentenced to imprisonment in 1913. In 1906 three Banks were founded, all of some importance,—the Bank of India (under important Parsee auspices), the Bank of Rangoon, and the Indian Specie Bank. Until 1910 these three Banks remained alone amongst the new creations in having a paid-up capital in excess of 15 lakhs (£100,000).[4] Since 1906 numerous Banks have been

[1] There is also, on a smaller scale, the Bangalore Bank (1868).

[2] There are a few others on a very small scale, such as the Kashmir Bank (1882), and the Poona Mercantile Bank (1893).

[3] In 1901 the People's Bank of India was founded, but it did not reach the 5 lakhs' limit until 1908.

[4] The Bank of India has a paid-up capital of 50 lakhs and a reserve and rest of 5½ lakhs; the corresponding figures for the Indian Specie Bank are 75

started, amongst the most important of which in respect of paid-up capital may be mentioned the Bengal National Bank (1907), the Bombay Merchants' Bank (1909), the Credit Bank of India (1909), the Kathiawar and Ahmedabad Banking Corporation (1910), and the Central Bank of India (1911).

The main object of most of these Banks is, of course, to attract deposits (though some of them are almost as much concerned at present with placing a further part of their unissued capital). For deposits fixed for a year the rate offered varies, as a rule, from 4½ to 5 per cent, the newer creations generally favouring the higher rate. Some Banks offer 6 per cent. About the rates for shorter periods there is more vagueness. On current accounts 2 per cent is generally allowed, though the eagerness of some of the newest Banks has led them to offer 2½. I have the advertisement before me of a Bank which offers 3 per cent on the daily balance, and up to 6 per cent on sums deposited for longer periods; at the head of the advertisement appears in large letters—Capital, Rs. 50,000,000; but it appears below that applications for shares are invited, and the paid-up capital is probably negligible. Some Banks advertise such advantages as "Special Marriage Deposits, 50 per cent added to Principal in five years' time."[1]

---

lakhs and 19 lakhs. The Bank of Rangoon is on a smaller scale and has been less successful.

[1] This represents compound interest at the rate of about 8 per cent per annum.

4½ per cent on deposits fixed for a year and 2 per cent on current accounts in excess of a certain minimum are very likely reasonable rates to offer in Indian conditions, provided that the funds thus attracted are not used for speculation and that adequate reserves are maintained in a liquid form. It is in this respect that the more substantial of these Banks are chiefly open to criticism. The official statistics are, unfortunately, very much out of date. But for the Banks which had a paid-up capital and reserve of at least 5 lakhs the available figures up to 1910 are as follows :—

INDIAN JOINT STOCK BANKS

	No. of Banks.	Capital, Reserve, and Rest.	Deposits.	Cash Balances.
1890	5	£340,000	£1,810,000	£370,000
1895	9	630,000	3,780,000	640,000
1900	9	850,000	5,380,000	790,000
1905	9	1,080,000	7,990,000	1,160,000
1906	10	1,270,000	7,700,000	1,000,000
1907	11	1,950,000	9,340,000	1,300,000
1908	14	2,060,000	10,840,000	1,630,000
1909	15	2,360,000	13,660,000	1,860,000
1910	16	2,510,000	17,110,000	1,870,000

22. These figures reveal, in my opinion, an exceedingly serious state of affairs. If they could be brought up to date, they would probably appear even worse. As late as 1900 these Banks were comparatively insignificant. Since that time they have succeeded in attracting so large a volume of deposits

as to make them an important part of the banking system of the country. Only six of them date back long enough to remember any real financial crisis in India (for the depression of 1907–8 was not accompanied by the symptoms of financial crisis). Growing up in smooth times, they have thought more of attracting deposits than of retaining cash reserves; and in 1910 we find sixteen Banks with deposits of £17,000,000 and cash reserves of not quite 11 per cent.[1] Even of these reserves the greater part is probably held by the older and more established of the Banks belonging to this class. In the case of the smaller Banks, dealing, as they are, with clients to whom banking is a new thing and in a country where hoarding is still dominant, the cash balances seem, from the available indications, to be hopelessly inadequate; and it is hard to doubt that in the next bad times they will go down like ninepins. If such a catastrophe occurs, the damage inflicted on India will be far greater than the direct loss falling on the depositors. The growth of banking habits in India is, of course, of the utmost importance to the country's economic development. A startling series of failures will do much to retard it.

In this connexion the history of the Bank of Burma, the first Bank of the new order to be founded, is instructive. This Bank was started in 1904 under European management by a firm engaged in floating

[1] Here again it is tantalising that no later figures should be available.

oil companies and other highly speculative enterprises. The Bank's capital was £117,500, and by 1911, when it failed, deposits had been attracted to the extent of £792,701, a large part of which is said to have come from Bombay and Calcutta. To obtain these deposits the Bank had offered interest at the rate of 6 per cent for deposits placed with it for a year; and many persons, it seems, were deceived by its title into believing that it was in some sense a Presidency Bank. In the autumn of 1911, after a year in which the Burma rice crop had been good and had sold at very high prices, and when the province generally was prosperous, the Bank failed. The balance sheet turned out to be false, and one-third of the assets had been advanced against worthless security to a firm in which the directors were interested.

23. Both in the case of the Exchange Banks and in that of the Indian Joint Stock Banks, the "Cash Balances" include, I think, balances held at other Banks.[1] It is impossible, therefore, to summarise accurately the figures for the Indian Banking System as a whole—Presidency Banks, Exchange Banks, and Joint Stock Banks together. The figures given below state accurately the total of private deposits; but in the total of cash balances some items must be counted twice over.

[1] In the official statistics no definition is given of what precisely is meant by "cash."

	Total Deposits in India, excluding Public Deposits.	Total Cash Balances.	Cash Per Cent of Deposits.
1890	£16,650,000	£11,310,000	68[1]
1895	19,430,000	7,570,000	39
1900	20,970,000	5,750,000	23
1905	34,230,000	9,150,000	27
1906	38,100,000	11,700,000	31
1907	40,880,000	11,350,000	28
1908	42,920,000	11,050,000	26
1909	48,930,000	12,430,000	25
1910	54,870,000	12,340,000	22

[1] An exceptional year.

The steady deterioration of the position, as shown in the above figures, is exceedingly marked. These figures flatter the Banks, rather than the reverse. For I have excluded the Public Deposits (amounting in 1910 to £2,820,000), and have included the whole of the cash balances (at the branches as well as the head offices) held by the Presidency Banks against them. If the figures could be worked out accurately, the present proportion of cash available against the private deposits would come out, I suspect, lower by far than appears superficially from the above table.

24. To complete the figures of Indian deposits,[1] it will be useful to give at this point the deposits in the Post Office Savings Banks, which have increased at a great rate, though not so fast as deposits in Banks, since 1900 :—

[1] The Co-operative Credit Societies are not important in this connexion, capital, reserves, loans, and deposits altogether being less than £1,000,000.

March 31.	Number of Depositors.	Deposits.
1900	785,729	£6,431,000
1905	1,058,813	8,938,000
1906	1,115,758	9,328,000
1907	1,190,220	9,845,000
1908	1,262,763	10,121,000
1909	1,318,632	10,156,000
1910	1,378,916	10,578,000
1911	1,430,451	11,279,000
1912[1]	1,500,834	12,599,000
1913[2]		13,860,000

[1] Limit of annual cash deposits raised from Rs. 200 to Rs. 500. [2] Estimate.

As in England, the Government do not maintain any specific reserve against these deposits. They are treated as unfunded debt and used for capital expenditure. It is important, therefore, to remember that the Government now hold in India nearly £14,000,000 of unfunded debt repayable at short notice to 1,500,000 depositors. This constitutes a not negligible claim on their general reserves.

25. The figures of the preceding paragraphs, in their cumulative effect, suggest the following reflection. Apart from any deterioration in the proportion of reserves held, the question of Indian deposits is now *important.* They stand for the first time at a figure which is large in relation to the total trade of the country and to the resources of the Government. If the Banks got into trouble, there will be much more far-reaching effects than could have been the case formerly. This is quite apart from the question whether they are more *likely* to get into trouble than

formerly. The question of the reserves they hold matters, therefore, more than it used. The information which I have been able to convey in this chapter is exceedingly incomplete. But, such as it is, it provides strong *prima facie* grounds for doubt and dissatisfaction.

26. The last group of Banks for discussion—since I have no precise *data* relating to the private and unincorporated bankers or money-lenders—consists of those numerous institutions registered as Banks under the Indian Companies Act, but with a capital insufficient or with activities too mixed for inclusion in the list of Indian Joint Stock Banks proper, dealt with above.

The available statistics (approximate) are as follows :—

March 31.	Number of Banks.	Paid-up Capital.
1900	398	£2,000,000
1905	510	2,200,000
1906	505	2,000,000
1907	504	1,900,000
1908	478	2,800,000
1909	492	3,100,000
1910	476	3,400,000

There are no statistics of their deposits. While the capital of these Banks has increased rather rapidly since 1907, the above figures show that it is not yet large.

Our interest in these Banks, however, arises not

so much out of the banking business which they may possibly transact, as out of certain, almost Gilbertian, characteristics calculated to bring the name and profession of banking into derision or disrepute. These Banks have discovered that there is, or may be, a useful ambiguity in the public mind between nominal capital and paid-up capital, and that nothing is cheaper than to increase the former. When, therefore, a Bank is registered, its promoters may just as well put down as its nominal capital sums ranging from £100,000 to £1,000,000 as anything else. One comic opera Bank registered in Calcutta in 1910 put down £20,000,000, without having at the time of the last return any paid-up capital at all. Apart from this exceptional venture, the 38 Banks registered in 1910–11 had between them a nominal capital of £1,306,000 and a paid-up capital of £19,500. With enormous nominal capitals they combine high-sounding titles—the Bank of Asia, the East India Bank, the Hindustan Bank, the United Bank of Commerce, and so forth. Once established, their activities are not limited. One of these Banks has included in its operations coach-building and medical attendance.

27. Plainly these ventures are not to be taken too seriously. But the recent activity of their promoters has raised some discussion in India as to whether it would not be for the public good to restrain them by legislation. In this matter, as is the case in so many

(her governors knowing no other model), the legislation of India has followed the lines of Great Britain's. Just as in this country there is no special law relating to the incorporation of Banks, so in India Banks are registered under the ordinary Joint Stock Companies Act. As a Bill to amend this Act has been to the front for some time, discussion has naturally centred round the question whether this opportunity should not be taken of introducing some suitable restrictions relating specifically to Banks.[1] While I am inclined to think that it would be more convenient to deal with this matter in a separate Bill, the important point is that decided action of some kind should be taken with the least possible delay. The Upper Indian Chamber of Commerce, in reply to an inquiry from Government in 1910, answered, very wisely, as follows:—

> The Committee feel very strongly that something more is needed (*i.e.*, than in other Companies) in the case of Banks where the capital and confidence, not only of the shareholders but of the depositors, are involved. New Banks are springing up with alarming rapidity, with little share capital subscribed; these Banks are trading on the confidence of the depositor who is little versed in money matters but is attracted by the name "Bank" and wishes to earn interest on his savings. . . . The fear is that if one of these mushroom growths fails, others will follow, and the timid depositor, unable to discriminate between the sound and the unsound concerns, will make haste to get his money back from whatever Bank it is in, and his confidence

[1] At the time of writing, this Bill has not yet passed through its final stages.

in banking institutions thus rudely checked will take years to win back.

Various suggestions have been made as to what restrictions would be proper. It has been proposed that it should not be permitted to combine banking operations with other businesses; that the accounts of Banks should be regularly audited and the results published; that fairly detailed accounts[1] should be published in the local official Gazette; that all institutions calling themselves Banks should be required to publish certain specified particulars at the head of every advertisement; and that capital and reserves should bear a certain proportion to liabilities before dividends may be paid. The abuse of a great disproportion between nominal and paid-up capital could be cured by a stamp duty on registration proportioned to the nominal capital. Provisions for due publicity will probably lead in the long-run to the best results—though care must be taken that the form for publication of accounts is well suited to bring to the light what is most relevant. Regulations of other kinds are apt to have hampering results which cannot be easily foreseen. During the infancy of Indian banking, nevertheless, it will very likely be wise to have some precise rule as to the kind and amount of the reserves.

28. In conclusion, something must be said about

[1] In the published balance sheet, which I have before me, of one of the largest of these little Banks, the cash is lumped together with the "investments," *i.e.*, with the Bank's speculations.

proposals for a State Bank. This is a proper subject for inquiry by a Royal Commission. I am not prepared to discuss it here in detail.

The question is an old one. In 1836 "a large body of merchants interested in the East Indies" submitted to the Court of Directors of the East India Company a project for a "great Banking Establishment for British India." Such a Bank, "confining its transactions strictly to Banking principles and business," and "established by Act of Parliament and possessed of adequate capital, would, under judicious management and control, become an instrument of general good by facilitating the employment of a portion of the redundant capital of this country (England) for the general improvement of Indian commerce, giving stability to the monetary system of India, and preventing those occasional fluctuations to which it is at present subject, and also by affording the Company facilities and advantages in their future financial arrangements." It was also to "facilitate the receipt of the revenue and its subsequent diffusion through the various channels of the public expenditure, furnish the remittance to Great Britain of the sums required there for the Home Charges, and enable the East India Company to act up to the instruction of the legislature by keeping their Government entirely aloof from that interference with the commerce of India which the present system of remittance involves. . . . At present the basis of the Bank of Bengal is too narrow for such a customer as the Government." I quote this from the *Account of the Presidency Banks* by Mr. J. B. Brunyate, who remarks on its appropriateness to present conditions. From 1860 to 1876 the possibility of the Bank of Bengal's developing into a "Bank of India" was constantly in the air, successive financial Members of Council being not unfriendly to the idea. In 1867 a specific proposal for the amalgamation of the three Presidency Banks was laid before the Government of India in a memorandum of complete grasp and mastery by Mr. Dickson, celebrated (in his own time) for pre-eminent ability as Secretary and Treasurer of the Bank of Bengal. The Viceroy's minute was unfavourable. "I submit," he wrote, "that it is not for the interest of a State that a great institution of the kind should grow up for all India, the interests of which may in time be opposed to those of the public, and whose influence at any rate may overshadow that of the Government itself. A Bank of such a character would be very difficult to manage. Few men in India would be found equal to the task. And as regards the interests and convenience of the merchants of Bombay and Madras, surely it is only natural that they should prefer separate Banks for those important centres of commerce." The Secretary of State's sole contribution to the discussion—no need to name him, it is the eternal Secretary of State speaking, not a transient individual—was as follows :—

> Any proposition for changes of a fundamental character, such as the establishment of a Central State Bank, or a return to the system of Government Treasuries, which may hereafter be taken into consideration, must be viewed in its general bearings, and not with special reference to the circumstances of a particular Presidency, or of a particular crisis.

The project was smothered in the magnificent and empty maxims of political wisdom.[1]

Before the Fowler Committee of 1898, there was some desultory discussion of proposals for a Central Bank of India, which were supported by a few of the witnesses; but, apart from Mr. Hambro's memorandum, no attempt was made to deal with the question in detail.[2]

29. At the present time the arguments in favour of a State Bank for India are very strong,—far stronger than they were in 1867 or even in 1898. The Government have taken over so many of the functions of a Central Bank, that they cannot wisely neglect the rest. A note issue of growing importance, the management of the Government's cash balances, the regulation of the foreign exchanges,—all these are controlled together and treated as a whole

[1] These quotations are derived from Mr. Brunyate's *Account*, *loc. cit.*

[2] In their Despatch dealing with the Report of the Fowler Committee (August 24, 1899) the Government of India went so far as to declare that the constitution of a State Bank, by the amalgamation and absorption of the three Presidency Banks, was desirable. For the circumstances and discussions which led up to the ultimate abandonment of these ideas, see "Papers relating to the Proposed Establishment of a Central Bank in India (reprinted from the *Gazette of India* and *Supplement*, dated the 12th Oct. 1901)."

in a compact and admirably conceived scheme. But other benefits cannot be obtained easily, so long as these functions are utterly divorced from those of banking proper. I summarise the arguments thus :—

(i.) The existing divorce between responsibility for the note issue and that for banking generally is contrary to modern banking practice, and is, in several respects, a source of weakness.

(ii.) In particular it leads to the keeping of two distinct reserves—the Government's reserves and the bankers' reserves—with no clearly defined relation between them, so that the reserves of the latter may be insufficient, without the assumption by the former of the fact or the machinery of responsibility.

(iii.) It leads also to a want of elasticity in the system, since in modern conditions this elasticity is most commonly provided by exactly that co-operation between banking and note issue which is lacking in India.

(iv.) The absence of a State Bank makes it difficult for the Government to use its cash balances or any other part of its liquid funds to the best advantage,—since it cannot prudently place the whole of its free resources in the hands of a private institution.

(v.) The absence of a central banking authority leads to a general lack of direction in the banking policy of the country: it is no one's business to look at the matter as a whole, to know the position of the market's component units, or to enforce prudence when it is needed. There is a multiple reserve system in theory, but hardly an adequate one in fact; and a danger exists that every one is reckoning, in a crisis, upon every one else.

(vi.) The absence of the advice and experience, which the officers of a State Bank would possess, is a source of weakness to Government itself. There are no high officials whose business it is to make finance the chief study of their life. The Financial Secretaryship is an incident in the career of a successful civilian. A Financial Member of Council is apt to come to the peculiar problems of his office with a fresh mind. Thus the financial officers of Government spend five years or so in mastering a difficult subject and have then reached a seniority which warrants promotion to duties of some other kind. So far as the Government of India is concerned, questions of finance and currency are in the hands of intelligent amateurs who begin with the timidity of ignorance and leave off just when they are becoming properly secure of their ground. It is not astonishing that the centre of power in these matters has tended to gravitate to the India Office and the India Council in London. For the officials and advisers of the Secretary of State have grown up in familiarity with the problems of Indian currency. Control from the India Office is always looked on, from an instinct often founded on wisdom, with jealousy and with suspicion; but in questions of currency they are likely, as things now are, to have the wider knowledge and experience. Yet the element of continuity supplied by the India Office — though, as I read the history of the last decade, it has been invaluable in guiding the evolution of the currency—is no proper solution of the difficulty. With Indian banking this authority cannot be adequately in touch, and it would be much better if trained experience were to be found in India herself. It is a remarkable thing that the two classical pronouncements on the fundamental problems of Indian Finance, which have stood the test of time—Mr. Dickson's, in 1867, on the question of a Central Bank, and Mr. A. M. Lindsay's, in 1878 and subsequently, on the regulation of a Gold Standard—should both have come from Secretaries of the Bank of Bengal, not from high officials of State. (Yet this last argument for a State Bank, though I have amplified it in my summary at greatest length, is not at all the most important. The arguments given first are those which govern the question.)

30. On the other hand, a fairly good case can be made out against a State Bank. Several of the defects, outlined above, could be remedied, in part at least, by less drastic proposals. The reasons on this side are mainly, nevertheless, those of conservatism and of caution (or timidity). The question, as soon as one attempts to frame practical suggestions, bristles with difficulties. The Government are naturally

afraid of so troublesome a proposal—and one so far removed from what they are used to; while there is no important body which is sufficiently interested in forcing it on their attention. The Banks fear a possible rival; merchants are content with present prosperity; and no one else knows anything about it. I shall be astonished, therefore, if action is taken while times are good. Perhaps we may have to wait for the lessons of a severe crisis. Only under some such strong influence as this is it likely that the responsible Government will nerve itself to the task, or the business community acquiesce in it.

31. If some day sufficient constructive energy is stirred into activity to undertake the task, let the framers of the new Bank's constitution put far from their minds all thoughts of the Bank of England. It is in the State Banks of Europe, especially in that of Germany, or in those, perhaps, of Holland or Russia, that the proper model is to be found.

CHAPTER VIII

THE INDIAN RATE OF DISCOUNT

1. THE Presidency Banks publish an official minimum rate of discount, in the same manner as the Bank of England. As an effective influence on the Money Market the Presidency Bank Rates do not stand, and do not pretend to stand, in a situation comparable in any respect with the Bank of England's. They do not attempt to control the market and to dictate what the rate ought to be. They, rather, follow the market and supply an index of the general position.

It is, therefore, as the best available index to variations in the value of money in India that the Presidency Bank Rates are chiefly interesting; and it is in this capacity that I shall make use of them in this chapter.

If we are to use these rates, however, as an index, a few warnings are first necessary. There is, of course, in India, just as there is in England, not one single rate for money, but several rates according to the period of the loan required (or the maturity of

Rate of Discount at the Presidency Bank of Bengal.

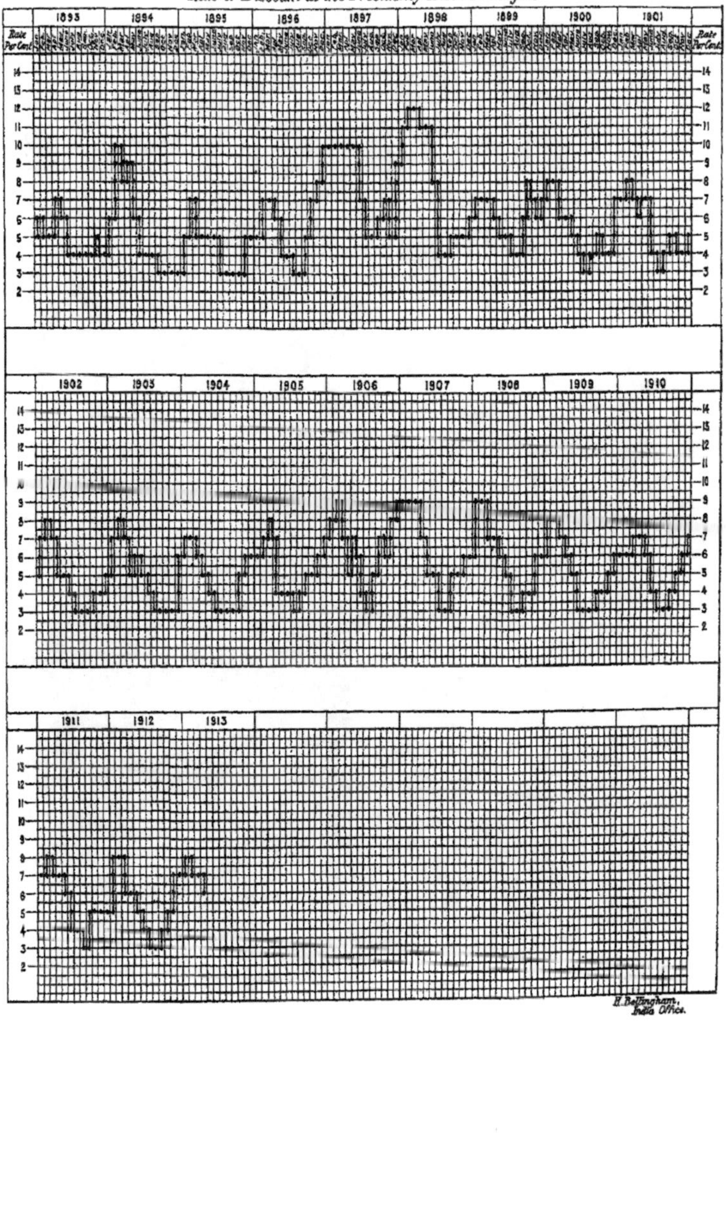

the bill negotiated) and the character of the security offered. The published Bank Rate in India represents, I believe, the rate charged day by day for a loan advanced on such security as Government Paper. The interest on a loan of this kind, that is to say, is calculated day by day at the published Bank Rate prevailing on each day. It may be said to correspond, therefore, to the London rate for some comparatively short period—say for fortnightly loans. Because the Bank Rate is at 7 per cent, it does not follow, therefore, that money can be used, or obtained, at this rate for two or three months. The rate ordinarily charged for fine bills of two or three months' currency may be either higher or lower than the published minimum Bank Rate. Further, the rates published by the Presidency Banks may be from time to time more or less "effective." The Banks may not always be able, that is to say, to do any considerable volume of business at their published minima. This would not be the case, I believe, in the busy season, so much as in the slack season, when the Banks do not let their published rates fall below 3 per cent, although money may be practically unusable and they would probably be glad enough to lend a large sum at 2 per cent. But those various qualifications do not prevent the Presidency Bank Rates from affording the best available index for measuring the relative ease or stringency of the Indian Money Market. I append a chart giving the movements of the Rate of

Discount at the Presidency Bank of Bengal since 1893.[1]

2. The rates, announced by the three Presidency Banks, are not always identical, but seldom, if ever, differ by more than 1 per cent. Such differences as there are chiefly reflect the differences in date at which occur the various crop movements with which each Presidency is mainly concerned. A wider difference of rate tends to be prevented, not only by the possibility of moving funds from one part of India to another, but also by the fact that the Secretary of State is willing to make his Bills and Transfers payable at any of the Presidency towns at the option of the purchaser. If there is relatively greater stringency at one of them, the bulk of the Council Bills and Transfers sold in London tend to be drawn on that one. The general appearance of the chart would not, therefore, have been appreciably different if I had chosen Bombay in place of Bengal.

The official rates move by one per cent at a time. There have been occasions of movements by 2 per cent, but not recently. When the rate is rising or falling, however, at the beginning or end of the busy season, changes often follow one another in quick succession.

3. An examination of the chart shows that the Indian Money Market enjoys years of high and low average rates respectively, just as other markets do. But these annual variations, while perfectly notice-

[1] I am indebted for the preparation of this chart to Mr. H. Bellingham of the India Office.

able, are relatively small in comparison with the seasonal changes, which are very great and very regular, and which afford the most clear ground of differentiation between the Indian Market and those with which we are familiar in Europe.

Let us examine the annual fluctuations of the rate in recent years in more detail :—

	Bengal Rate per Cent.			Bengal Rate per Cent.	
	Max. rate in February.	Min. rate in August.		Max. rate in February.	Min. rate in August.
1900	8	3	1907	9	3
1901	8	3	1908	9	3
1902	8	3	1909	8	3
1903	8	3	1910	6	3
1904	7	3	1911	8	3
1905	7	3	1912	8	3
1906	9	3	1913	8	

From this table and the chart it is safe to make the generalisation that the Indian Rate may be expected to reach 8 per cent in the winter or early spring, and to fall to 3 per cent in summer. Years differ from one another chiefly in the length of time for which the high and low rates prevail respectively. From 8 to 3 per cent is an enormous range for the normal seasonal fluctuation. What is the explanation of it? The Bank of England rate seldom exceeds 5 per cent, and in many years falls short of this, even in the winter. If there is so regular an expectation of obtaining 7 or 8 per cent in India on excellent security, why is it not worth some one's while to transfer funds to India in the busy season on an ampler scale than is the case at present, and thus secure the advantage of so wide a discrepancy between the English and the Indian rates?

4. The facts are to be explained, I think, as follows. High rates of 7 or 8 per cent are not obtainable in India all the year round. In normal years they cannot be relied on to prevail for more than about three months. The banker who raises funds in London in order to lend them for short periods in India has to choose between leaving them in India all the year round, waiting after one busy season for the next, and bringing them back again to London after a comparatively short period. He must either accept, that is to say, the rate obtainable in India on the average of the whole year, or he must earn a high enough rate in the brief busy season to compensate him for bearing the expense of remittance *both ways*.

In considering the difference between two European Bank Rates as the cause of a transfer of funds between the two centres, the cost of remittance, as measured by the difference between the telegraphic rate of exchange outwards at the beginning of the transaction and the telegraphic rate of exchange back at the end of it, is not, of course, to be neglected. But where the two centres are near together and there is no reason to anticipate the suspension of a free market in gold, this cost is, relatively, a minor consideration. The great distance, however, between London and India makes it in their case a very significant quantity, and a brief calculation shows that, measured in terms of Bank Rate, the cost of remittance works out higher, perhaps, than uninstructed common sense would anticipate. For, under present conditions, the cost of remittance both ways can hardly be less than $\frac{1}{16}$d. per rupee, rising in most years as between certain dates as high as $\frac{5}{32}$d., and reaching occasionally as much as $\frac{3}{16}$d. It would not be prudent to act on the expectation of a less cost than $\frac{3}{32}$d. Now $\frac{3}{32}$d. on a rupee is about ·6 per cent. If this loss on exchange (*i.e.* on remittance) is to be recouped in three months (*i.e.* in a quarter of a year), an additional rate of nearly $2\frac{1}{2}$ per cent per annum must be earned in India as compared with the rate in London. If a different degree of loss in exchange is anticipated, and if the length of time for which money can be used in India at a high rate is expected to be more or less than three months, the calculation must be adjusted accordingly. In any case the reason why the Indian and London Bank Rates can differ from one another for short periods by large amounts is adequately explained. If, for example, money can be employed in India at the high rate for one month only, even if the double cost of remittance for that period is so low as $\frac{1}{16}$d., the difference between the London and Indian rates must amount to 5 per cent per annum to make a transfer of funds *prima facie* profitable.

These illustrations show that what seems a very small fluctuation in exchange can account for a very wide difference in the rate of discount; and, apart from questions of unequal knowledge and unequal security, it is this possibility of fluctuation that makes distinct markets of the two centres. The underlying explanation is essentially the same as that of the circumstance to which I called attention in § 9 of Chapter II., namely, that a temporary premium of $\frac{3}{4}$ per cent on gold in those European countries where gold is not always freely obtainable, is as effective as a very great increase in the Bank Rate in preventing the remittance of funds abroad and even in attracting an inward flow of funds.

5. This discussion will have served to make clear a distinction highly important to the problem of the Indian Bank Rate. When we say that the Indian Bank Rate is apt to be high, we mean, not that the *average* effective rate over the whole year is high, but that the *maximum* rate in each year, effective for periods of shorter or longer duration, is generally high. A high average rate and a high maximum rate are likely to call for different explanations and, if a remedy is sought, for different kinds of remedies. The available evidence does not suggest that the average rate in India is at all unduly high for a country in India's stage of economic and financial development. Some of the Exchange Banks, for example, do not find it worth their while to offer

more than $3\frac{1}{2}$ per cent on Indian deposits fixed for a year. It is the high maximum rate almost invariably reached which calls for enquiry.

The phenomenon under discussion is in no way peculiar to India and does not arise out of those features of the Indian system which are characteristic of a Gold-Exchange Standard. We find the same thing in any country where the demand for funds for financing trade is to a high degree seasonal and variable in amount throughout the year, and where, at the same time, these funds have to be remitted from some far distant foreign centre—in the countries of South America, for example. In fact, by the establishment of a par of exchange between the rupee and sterling, the severity of seasonal stringency has been greatly moderated. The exceptionally high Bank Rates of 1897 and 1898 were partly occasioned by a natural timidity on the part of the Banks in importing funds at a rate of exchange which at that time was exceptionally high. The Banks had no guarantee that exchange would be maintained at or near the existing level, and if they imported funds they ran the risk of having to bring them home again at a heavy loss. Under present arrangements the maximum fluctuation in exchange between the busy season and the slack is known and limited. But while the stabilisation of the gold value of the rupee has done much for the Indian Money Market, and has rendered a 12 per cent Bank Rate most improbable except at a time of widespread crisis and panic, it does not prevent an 8 per cent or even a 9 per cent Bank Rate from being a comparatively common occurrence. Is it possible to conceive of any remedy or moderating influence for the somewhat severe seasonal stringency still experienced?

6. It is clear that a remedy can be sought in one or other of two ways only. Either the cost of remittance and the maximum range of fluctuation in exchange must be reduced, or a new source for the seasonal supply of funds must be found in India herself. I will discuss these alternatives in turn.

It will help to make the points at issue plain if I begin by taking an extreme case. Let us suppose that exchange between London and Calcutta were fixed at 1s. 4d., in the sense that the Government were always prepared to provide telegraphic remittance *in either direction* at this rate. Under such circumstances, the London and Indian Money Markets would become practically one market, and the large differences which can now exist between rates current in the two centres for loans on similar security would become impossible. The effect of this on the volume of remittance would be very great. Every year immense sums would be remitted from London to India in the busy season and brought back again at the end of it, since the fact which now diminishes the profitableness of such transactions would have ceased to exist. The following illustration shows on how large a scale these seasonal movements to and fro would probably be. In July the cash reserves of the Bank of Bengal might stand, as things now are, at, let us suppose, about 1000 lakhs and its discount rate at 3 per cent. This reserve might be 400 or 500 lakhs at least in excess of what prudence required. But it would be useless to lower the Bank Rate; for the additional funds were probably not loanable in India for the month of July at any rate at all. Yet for the reasons already given it would not be worth while in existing circumstances for any one to borrow this sum and remit it to London, until such time as it may be again wanted in Calcutta;—it is better to let it lie idle and wait for busier times. But fix exchange at 1s. 4d. and all this would be changed. The Bank's customers would immediately remit the 400 or 500 lakhs to London, knowing that they could be brought back without loss as soon as they were wanted. Every one in India having loanable funds to spare would act likewise.

What would be the effect on the Secretary of State if he were to lay himself under such an obligation? In order to be in a position to act as universal money-changer, and to be able to provide large quantities of sterling in London in the slack season, and large quantities of rupee funds in India in the busy season, it would be necessary for him to keep very much larger reserves than he does at present in both countries. It might even be necessary for him to remit gold backwards and forwards himself, thus bearing the whole expense of which the Exchange Banks were being relieved. At present the possible fluctuation of exchange between what may fairly be termed the "gold points" on either side of 1s. 4d., acts in some measure as a protection to the currency and lessens the reserves which it is necessary for the authorities to maintain; a falling exchange acts as a drag on remittance from India and a rising exchange as a drag on remittance from London, thus bringing the private interests of individuals and the natural forces acting on the market into greater harmony with the interests of the market as a whole, and with the efforts of the Secretary of State to maintain the stability of the system. If telegraphic exchange were fixed at 1s. 4d., the Indian Bank Rate would closely follow London's, but it would be at the expense of forcing the Secretary of State enormously to increase his reserves.

7. I have taken this extreme case in order to make emphatic the principles involved in all such proposals. But no one is likely to propose the above as a practical policy. More moderate proposals of the same kind, however, deserve consideration. Some critics, for example, have suggested that the Secretary of State should never sell Council Bills in London below 1s. 4d. This would lessen to a certain extent the probable range of fluctuation in exchange and might, therefore, diminish the risk of loss involved in remitting to India when exchange is high; but

the Secretary of State's withdrawal from the market would not necessarily prevent exchange from falling below 1s. 4d. Moreover, in normal times the policy actually followed already approximates closely to this proposal; in the last three years the occasions on which Council Bills have been sold below 1s. 4d. have been very rare. And in exceptional times it may be some protection to the sterling reserves if Council Bills can be sold at a lower rate if necessary. I conclude, therefore, that the advantage of such a policy would not be great, probably not great enough to outweigh the cost.

Thus it is not easy to find a remedy for high Bank Rate by any method of diminishing the maximum range of fluctuation in exchange. Indeed so long as the currency arrangements are at all like those now in force, this maximum range may fairly be said to be determined by forces outside Government control, namely, by the forces governing the cost of remittance of gold. Though the burden of this cost may be shifted, it cannot be easily avoided altogether.

8. We must fall back, therefore, on the second alternative, the discovery of a new source for the seasonal supply of funds in India herself. A proposal, having this object in view, has already been put forward in more than one passage in the preceding pages. I believe that, in future, the Government of India may have in the busy season a considerable stock of rupee funds available in the

Paper Currency Reserve and, occasionally, a surplus stock in the Indian Cash Balances. If a proper machinery is set up for lending these out in India, I anticipate some appreciable relief to the Bank Rate at the season of greatest stringency. Assuming that such a policy is practicable on other grounds, let us try to compare its precise effect as compared with the existing state of affairs.

9. Broadly speaking, surplus Government funds in India can at present be released only by the sale of Council Bills in London. When these bills are sold at a fairly high rate, the Government gain the premium over and above 1s. 4d. and are in a position to put out at interest funds in London. If the funds in India, instead of being released through the encashment of Council Bills, are lent out there direct, the interest obtained in India takes the place of the two sources of gain distinguished above. In the first case money is first borrowed from the London Money Market (by the Exchange Banks or otherwise) for the purchase of Council Bills, and is then lent back again to that Market by the Secretary of State. In the second case, instead of a double transaction in London there is a single transaction in India. It might be argued that the two methods come in the end to much the same thing; that there can be no relief to the Money Market unless the Government of India accept a lower rate of interest for sums lent out in India than is the equivalent of what they

would make if they were to sell Council Bills at a premium and lend out the funds in England; and that the second method involves no net addition to the resources available in India. For the following reasons, however, I do not think that this way of looking at the matter would be correct.

In the first place there would be an elimination of risk. If the average loss from exchange on funds sent out to India for the busy season works out at (say) 2 per cent per annum, the Banks, in order to recompense themselves for the risk of fluctuations beyond the average, would be able to make a difference of more than 2 per cent between the current Indian and English rates. In the case of funds borrowed in terms of rupees and repayable in terms of rupees, this element of risk is absent; and the elimination of it provides a source of net gain. If the effect of Government lending in India were to mitigate the seasonal stringency there, some lowering of the normal upper limit of fluctuation of exchange might result. In so far as this was the case, in normal years the consequences would be outwardly similar to those of the first alternative, discussed and rejected above, whilst the Government would not have bound themselves by any undertaking capable of turning out burdensome.

Secondly, the rate of interest which the Secretary of State can earn on loans in London is appreciably lower, on account of the short period for which he lends and the nature of the security he requires, than the normal rate at which the Exchange Banks would raise their funds there, and a good deal lower than what would be obtained by direct lending in India. (It should be admitted, on the other hand, that the practice of lending funds in India would probably involve some sacrifice of perfect safety as compared with the present arrangements.)

And, thirdly, it is not clear that it might not sometimes be feasible to lend out in India sums additional to those which would in fact be released under the present system, so that there would be some net addition to the resources available in India.

10. In addition, therefore, to the grounds for making loans in India from the Paper Currency Reserve which I have given in earlier chapters, I believe that it is in this direction that the best hope lies of a remedy for the high level which the Indian Bank Rate commonly reaches in the course of each busy season. I do not feel in a position to say anything very decided as to the manner in which such loans could be best made. But there is a presumption, I think, that, in the absence of a State Bank, they must be made, mainly if not entirely, through the Presidency Banks. And I believe that the Government would act advisedly if, as a general rule, 5 or 5½ per cent were the highest rate they ever chose to exact from the Banks. In financial matters of this kind there is a danger lest Governments prove

too jealous of the profits of private persons. In a case where the co-operation of private persons is necessary, they must be allowed a reasonable share of the profits of the transaction. In their past relations with the Presidency Banks in the matter of temporary loans, the Government of India have sometimes seemed to attach more importance to preventing the Banks from making any profit out of the loans than to any other aspect of the transaction. I may repeat that the loans I contemplate are to be for the busy season only, and that they should not be made until the expectation of a normal or successful harvest is reasonably assured.

11. In the nature of a postscript to the above proposals, it may be instructive to consider them in the light of the actual circumstances of the season 1912–13. The peculiarity of this season from the point of view of the Indian Money Market was the combination of a high Bank Rate in India for a comparatively long period[1] with a relatively low rate of exchange and only a moderate demand for Council Bills and gold. At the end of 1912 the situation could have been described as normal. The Bank Rate was at the somewhat high level usual at that time of year; exchange was high (the minimum rate for the allotment of Council Bills being 1s. $4\frac{3}{32}$d.); and the demand for Council Bills was on a large scale.

[1] The Bengal Bank Rate was at 7 or 8 per cent from November 28, 1912, to April 17, 1913, and the Bombay Bank Rate at no less than 8 per cent from December 27, 1912, to April 3, 1913.

But from January to March, although the Bank Rate remained at a high level and trade was active, the demand for Council Bills fell away, slowly at first and rapidly during March, exchange dropping *pari passu* until, during the latter half of March, the minimum rate at which Council Bills were allotted fell so low as 1s. $3\frac{3}{4}\frac{1}{2}$d. The combination of so low a rate of exchange with an 8 per cent Bank Rate at Bombay was very abnormal.

It is dangerous for a writer who is not in touch with the practical side of the Money Market to venture on an explanation of current events. But I will give my explanation for what it is worth. The poor demand for Council Bills in March 1913 is not to be explained by the competition of gold as a means of remittance; for the low level of exchange did not favour the importation of sovereigns (even from Egypt, except earlier in the season), and as a matter of fact the import of them was on a very much smaller scale than in the previous year. It must have been due, therefore, to an unwillingness on the part of the Exchange Banks and others to lay out money in London for the purchase of remittance to India. This unwillingness was due to a variety of causes. The lock-up of funds in silver and opium, and the freedom with which India was purchasing foreign goods, probably had something to do with it; and an important contributory influence was the dearness[1] of money in

[1] The Bank of England's rate was 5 per cent, with the market rate well

London combined with a sufficient expectation of cheaper money soon, to provide an incentive to delay, wherever delay was possible. A precise diagnosis of the causes of the unwillingness on the part of the Banks to buy Council Bills is not necessary, however, to the lesson I seek to enforce. For whatever reason, Indian Bank Rates of 7 and 8 per cent, even in combination with a very low level of exchange, did not in fact tempt the Banks to buy Council Bills on any considerable scale. What was the effect on the Government Balances in India? The ordinary method, by which the rupees accumulating in the Reserve Treasuries from the proceeds of taxation are quickly released and given back to the Money Market, the encashment, namely, of large volumes of Council Bills, had failed. The position was aggravated by the large realised surplus, much of which was to be devoted to expenditure only in the *next* financial year, and which in the meantime was swelling the Government Balances in any case beyond their usual dimensions. So far, therefore, from assisting the market, the Government were busy increasing the stringency by taking off the market, week by week, rupees which for the moment they did not in the least want. Already at the end of 1912 (see table on p. 188) the sums lying idle in the Reserve Treasuries were unusually high.

up to the Bank Rate; and the *difference* between the current rates for money in London and India was probably, for the time of year, not much greater than usual.

By the end of February 1913, the total Government Balances in India had risen to £17,400,000, and by the end of March to £19,300,000, of which £8,000,000 lay in the Reserve Treasuries. What Money Market in the world could have seen such sums taken out of its use and control at one of the busiest moments of the year without suffering a loss of ease?

The situation was not due, in my judgment, to any ignorance or incompetence on the part of the executive officers of Government, but to a system which provided them with no sort of appropriate machinery for dealing with the position. The "Independent Treasury System" and the traditional aloofness of Government from the Money Market were seen at their worst. Millions of rupees were lying idle in the Government Treasuries at the time of year when there was most work for them to do outside. The sort of arrangements I have outlined in earlier paragraphs might have done something, I feel sure, to ease the situation. One can point, therefore, to the first quarter of 1913 as a specific occasion on which Government could have lent sums in India with profit to itself, with advantage to the Money Market, and without incurring any risk of which it need have been afraid.

12. I have now completed my discussion of these questions. Two points I would end by emphasising. The first affects my general treatment of the subject matter. I have tried to bring out the fact that the Indian system is an exceedingly *coherent* one. Every

part of the system fits into some other part. It is impossible to say everything at once, and an author must needs sacrifice from time to time the complexity and interdependence of fact in the interests of the clearness of his exposition. But the complexity and the coherence of the system require the constant attention of anyone who would criticise the parts. This is not a peculiarity of Indian Finance. It is the characteristic of all monetary problems. The difficulty of the subject is due to it.

My second point affects the kinship of Indian arrangements to those lately developed in other parts of the world. Indian affairs are so exclusively studied by those whose knowledge and experience is preponderantly Indian or English, that the true perspective of India's development is sometimes lost; and the value of foreign experiences neglected. I urge that, in her Gold-Exchange Standard, and in the Mechanism by which this is supported, India, so far from being anomalous, is in the forefront of monetary progress. But in her banking arrangements, in the management of her note issue, and in the relations of her Government to the Money Market, her position *is* anomalous; and she has much to learn from what is done elsewhere.

INDEX

THE END